D0828973

Blessings That Make Us Be

To Bruce

May you be blessed &
be a blessing to
others,

Susan A Muto

2000

Adrian van Kaam

ALSO AVAILABLE FROM SAINT BEDE'S PUBLICATIONS

Pathways of Spiritual Living, 1984

Songs for Every Season
(with Adrian van Kaam and Richard Byrne), 1989

BLESSINGS
THAT MAKE US BE

*A Formative Approach
to Living the Beatitudes*

Susan Annette Muto

SAINT BEDE'S PUBLICATIONS
Petersham, Massachusetts 01366

Saint Bede's Publications
Saint Scholastica Priory
P.O. Box 545, North Main Street
Petersham, MA 01366-0545

Copyright 1982 by Susan Annette Muto

All rights reserved. No part of this book may be reproduced, stored in a retrieval system, or transmitted, in any form or by any means, electronic, mechanical, photocopying, recording or otherwise, without the written permission of Saint Bede's Publications.

PRINTED IN THE UNITED STATES OF AMERICA

97   96   95   94   93   92   91   6   5   4   3   2

LIBRARY OF CONGRESS CATALOGING IN PUBLICATION DATA
Muto, Susan Annette. Blessings that make us be.
1. Beatitudes. 2. Christian Life — Catholic authors.
I. Title.
BT382.M88   1982   241.5'3   82-13102
ISBN 0-932506-88-7

An Irish Blessing

May the blessing of light be with you—
Light outside and light within.
May sunlight shine upon you and warm your heart 'til it glows
   like a peat fire,
So that the stranger may come and warm himself by it.

May the blessed light shine out of your two eyes
Like a candle set in two windows of the house
Bidding the wanderer to come in out of the storm.
May you ever give a kindly greeting to those whom
You pass as you go along the road.

May the blessings of rain—the sweet, soft rain—
   fall upon you,
So that little flowers may spring up to shed
   their sweetness in the air.

May the blessings of the earth—the good rich earth—
   be with you,
May the earth be soft under you when you rest on it,
   Tired at the end of the day.
May the earth rest easy over you when at last
   you lie under it.
May the earth rest so lightly over you that your spirit
May be out from under it quickly, and on its way to God.

Contents

Foreword

This book on the Beatitudes by Dr. Susan Annette Muto is a beautiful contribution to the articulation of the science of foundational human formation in the Christian formation tradition.

The first book dealing with articulation research to be published by Crossroad was written by Dr. Carolyn Gratton, associate professor at the Institute of Formative Spirituality. Her outstanding contribution was an illustration of how a specific scientific field, in her case counseling psychology, can be articulated in light of the science of formation.

This contribution by Dr. Muto, a director and professor at the same institute, is a striking example of how a basic theme of the Christian formation tradition can be articulated in light of the same science.

Dr. Muto deserves our appreciation for reawakening our interest in these foundational attitudes. As Dr. Gratton has done in her field, she has succeeded admirably in making familiar Christian themes appear new in light of the science of foundational human formation.

Adrian van Kaam

Preface

The Sermon on the Mount in Matthew's Gospel begins with the Beatitudes.[1] It is one of the most read and commented upon sections of the Bible. The Fathers of the Church quote it more than any other chapter. This wealth of commentary would seem to indicate that the Sermon offers a classical statement pertaining to the foundations of Christian formation.

It has, of course, raised many historical, political, exegetical, social, and theological questions around which center various schools of interpretation, both pre- and post-Reformation. For example, the Beatitudes have been read as absolute and literal directives; as commonsense intentions to be modified in accordance with one's situation; as hyperbolic statements made to highlight the radical demands of an imminent eschaton; as general principles grounded in the consciousness that God is our All in all.[2]

Our task in this formative reading is not to debate with these various interpretations. While taking them into account, we want to approach the Beatitudes in light of the science of foundational human formation.[3] This science, founded and developed by Adrian van Kaam and his colleagues and students, seeks to disclose, via reflection on our formative experiences, the basic or foundational dynamics, structures, and conditions for living a harmonious spiritual and social life. The Beatitudes offer such conditions. They also communicate directives that must be incarnated in daily life if we want to live fully our commitment to Christ.

In this formative reading of the Beatitudes, we intend to treat these eight directives as "be-attitudes."[4] In them, the Lord tells us how to be in such a way that our lives reflect the formation mys-

tery unfolding in and around us.[5] He shows us a path of formation by which we can become fully human and Christian, less
ego-centered and more centered in the Divine Will for us. These
attitudes are not pious words but invitations to transform our inner lives. From this intraformation, we can bring new hope and
life to others in inter- and outerformation.[6]

The Beatitudes dispose us to be open to the presence of God
within us so that our Christian attitudes of social justice, peace,
and mercy may flow over in daily acts of congenial, compatible,
and compassionate love and service.[7] Living the Beatitudes thus
tempers what Adrian van Kaam calls the power of the pride form
and facilitates the release of the Christ form in us.[8]

When we live inspired by the formative power of the Beatitudes, they evoke in us a renewed appreciation of the doctrines
and directives of our faith, of its truth and beauty. Because the
Beatitudes are attitudes of being, they are grounded in human nature. They connote as well a natural religious meaning that is ex-
panded and deepened in light of the Christian revelation. Implicit
in each Beatitude is also a message pertaining to practical formation, that is, to the awareness of obstacles that may block the flow
of grace in our being and of conditions that facilitate its release so
that our hearts and lives may become more and more Christ-like.

Thus, as we ponder the formative meaning of each Beatitude,
we shall follow this pattern: First, we shall consider the anthro-
pological rooting of the Beatitude insofar as this attitude tells us
something of foundational validity for all human beings. Our
guiding question will be: What does this Beatitude mean in terms
of foundational human formation?

Second, we shall consider the Beatitude in light of the religious
articulations of mankind that for the most part predate the Christian revelation. Our guiding question here will be: What does this
Beatitude tell us about the basic orientation of the human being as
spirit to go beyond, to seek for the More Than, to aspire toward
the Transcendent or Sacred Other in whatever way the Divine is
understood by one's religious formation tradition?

Third, we shall enter into the formative meaning of the Beatitude proper to Christian revelation and its consequent articulation
in the Christian formation tradition. We will see that behind these
words stands the Person of Jesus, who himself is the fullness of

the experiences out of which he preached to the people. For who sorrowed more than he? Who was more merciful? Whose poverty and self-emptying could have been greater?

Finally, we shall suggest some practical applications of each Beatitude, beginning with a consideration of obstacles that hinder our formation. These obstacles, when overcome by the help of grace, may become gifted openings that facilitate the release of the Christ form of our soul.

A further division of the Beatitudes that will foster our formative approach follows the traditional threefold path of the mystical way—the path of purgation, illumination, and union. Certain Beatitudes seem to be based in experiences that are purifying and potentially transforming. We refer here to the Purgative Beatitudes of mourning; hunger and thirst; and persecution. As we grow more like the Divine Master, who teaches these truths, we are able to be gentle, more merciful, and at peace. These Christ-like attitudes increasingly illumine our inner being and affect our outer actions. Therefore the Beatitudes pertaining to mercifulness, gentleness, and peacemaking can be called the Illuminative Beatitudes. As we grow in these dispositions, we may experience the joy of intimate union with the Indwelling Trinity. Like Jesus, we are poor in spirit and pure of heart. In our humility, we may experience a new advent of trust and confidence in the Lord. In our simplicity, we may enjoy the gift of seeing the invisible splendor of the mystery of divine formation. God may grace us with unceasing prayer and enable us to experience the peace and joy of the unitive life. Thus the Beatitudes pertaining to poverty of spirit and purity of heart can be called the Unitive Beatitudes.

After the two opening chapters on foundations for living and reading the Beatitudes formatively, the book is divided into three major sections pertaining to the Purgative Beatitudes (mourning; hunger and thirst; persecution); the Illuminative Beatitudes (mercy; meekness; peacemaking); and the Unitive Beatitudes (poverty of spirit; purity of heart). Together, these Beatitudes lead us through the desert of purgation to the valley of illumination onto the heights of union. Each Beatitude tells us something about who we are and who we can become if we heed the directives issued layer upon layer in these formative words.

In this journey through the Beatitudes, we shall try to be faithful to the intention expressed so well by St. Augustine in his commentary on the Sermon on the Mount. He wrote that the discourse delivered by the Lord is "the perfect pattern of the Christian life" and that it is "made up of all the precepts by which the Christian life has vitality."[9]

The Beatitudes can thus be compared to eight keys that unlock the treasures of Christian formation. These attitudes intend a community of persons not tormented by oppressive imperatives but loved into freedom by God. These directives are not a record of legislation but of love. The Beatitudes, like the Gospels themselves, proceed by the "logic of extravagance."[10] This means that they direct us paradoxically by disorienting and surprising us. They make us attentive to limit-experiences like suffering and death. They call for a decision.

In other words, we are led by them to consider previously unconsidered possibilities for transcendent formation. They dislocate us for the sake of relocating us in a new range of possible attitudes and actions.[11] By leading us to the breaking point of mere logic, they allow us to break through to the logic of extravagance—to that logic by which a shepherd abandons ninety-nine sheep to save one. As keys to the divinely forming mystery, the Beatitudes invite us to explore new avenues of inner liberation. They move us by means of a dialectic of proclamation and promise. The Lord blesses who we are here and now and promises us how much more we shall become.[12] To respond to these blessings is to fulfill the universal call to holiness proclaimed by the Church as the graced goal of all Christian formation.

Notes

1. The Beatitudes mark the opening of the Sermon on the Mount. In this book, I am using the rendition according to St. Matthew. The titles of each chapter are taken from the Revised Standard Version of the Bible, in which the following text appears:

> Seeing the crowds, he went up on the mountain, and when he sat down his disciples came to him. And he opened his mouth and taught them saying:

> > *"Blessed are the poor in spirit, for theirs*
> > *is the kingdom of heaven.*

> *"Blessed are those who mourn, for they shall be comforted.*
> *"Blessed are the meek, for they shall inherit the earth.*
> *"Blessed are those who hunger and thirst for righteousness, for they shall be satisfied.*
> *"Blessed are the merciful, for they shall obtain mercy.*
> *"Blessed are the pure in heart, for they shall see God.*
> *"Blessed are the peacemakers, for they shall be called sons of God.*
> *"Blessed are those who are persecuted for righteousness' sake, for theirs is the kingdom of heaven.*
>
> (*Mt. 5: 1–11*)

See Herbert G. May and Bruce M. Metzger, eds., *The Oxford Annotated Bible with the Apocrypha*, Revised Standard Version (New York: Oxford University Press, 1965), pp. 1175–76. All other biblical quotations in this book are taken from *The New American Bible* (Camden, N.J.: Catholic Publishers, 1971).

2. In the Roman Catholic tradition, a distinction is made between the Beatitudes, as precepts for everyone, and the evangelical counsels, to which only some explicitly vow themselves. In the Protestant tradition, one finds the Lutheran view that the Beatitudes operate on two planes simultaneously, the spiritual and the temporal; the view of Schweitzer, who looks upon the Beatitudes as an "interim ethic"; the modern dispensationalist view promoted in the Scofield Bible; the repentance view in reformed thought; and the unconditional divine will view of Dibelius, which holds that God's will is absolute and that the disciple is responsible for any deviations. See Warren S. Kissinger, *The Sermon on the Mount: A History of Interpretation and Bibliography* (Metuchen, N.J.: Scarecrow Press, 1975); and Harvey K. McArthur, *Understanding the Sermon on the Mount* (Westport, Conn.: Greenwood Press, 1960).

3. See Adrian van Kaam, "Editor's Note," *Studies in Formative Spirituality* 3 (1982): 7–11. The author observes that this journal and its publisher, the Institute of Formative Spirituality at Duquesne University, Pittsburgh, Pennsylvania, are "not only concerned with the science of foundational human formation but also with complementing its research in this field by 'articulation research,' in this case especially in terms of the Christian formation tradition." See Adrian van Kaam, *Formative Spirituality,* vol. 1 (New York, Crossroad Publishing Co., 1982).

4. See George L. Lawlor, *The Beatitudes Are for Today* (Grand Rapids, Mich.: Baker Book House, 1974): and Father Ray Roh, *Beatitudes: Blueprints for Christian Living* (Pecos, N.M.: Dove Publications, 1978).

5. See Adrian van Kaam, "Christian Ideal Life Form as Final Means of Ultimate Fulfillment in Christ," a description found in his "Provisional Glossary of the Terminology of the Science of Foundational Formative Spirituality," *Studies in Formative Spirituality* 1 (1980): 294. Hereafter abbreviated *G, Studies* following the first full reference to this journal in each chapter.

6. See Adrian van Kaam, "Explanatory Charts of the Science of Foundational

Formation," G, *Studies* 2 (1981): 127–43. An explanation of "The Formation-Polarity Diagram" and the "Polarity Chart" itself can be found on pp. 130 and 140, respectively.

7. ". . . congeniality, compatibility and compassion . . . give rise to justice, peace and mercy." See Adrian van Kaam, "Social Effects of this Transforming Union," G, *Studies* 2 (1981): 516.

8. "True formation, fulfillment and self-exertion are only possible when we rise beyond this ignorance of the autarchic pride form and participate in the Mystery of Formation. . . ." See Adrian van Kaam, "Dominance of the Autarchic Pride Form," G, *Studies* 1 (1980): 459. See also "Invisible Revealed Obstacles to Consonant Formation Appraisal and Decision," G, *Studies* 1 (1980): 473.

9. St. Augustine, "The Lord's Sermon on the Mount," trans. John J. Jepson, *Ancient Christian Writers: The Works of the Fathers in Translation* (Westminster, Md.: The Newman Press, 1948). See also St. Gregory of Nyssa, "The Lord's Prayer, The Beatitudes," trans. Hilda C. Graef, *Ancient Christian Writers: The Works of the Fathers in Translation* (New York: The Newman Press, 1954).

10. Paul Ricoeur writes, "In most of the parables of Jesus there is an element of extravagance which alerts and summons our attention" (p. 244). He deals with this "logic of extravagance" in an essay published in *The Philosophy of Paul Ricoeur: An Anthology of His Work,* ed. Charles E. Reagan and David Stewart (Boston: Beacon Press, 1978), pp. 239–45.

11. See Rosemary Haughton, *Transformations of Man: A Study of Conversion and Community* (Springfield, Ill.: Templegate, 1967). Chapter 1, "Conflict and Resolution," discusses the dynamics of formation and Christian transformation in everyday situations.

12. See, especially, Simon Tugwell, *The Beatitudes: Soundings in Christian Traditions* (Springfield, Ill.: Templegate, 1980); William Barclay, *The Beatitudes and The Lord's Prayer for Everyman* (New York: Harper & Row, 1963); and Michael H. Crosby, *Spirituality of the Beatitudes* (New York: Orbis Books, 1981).

Acknowledgments

I would like to say a word of profound thanks to my colleagues at the Institute of Formative Spirituality at Duquesne University, most notably to our founder and Director Emeritus, Father Adrian van Kaam, C.S.Sp., Ph.D., whose pioneering work in the science of foundational human formation and its religious and Christian articulation has provided the main guidelines for my approach to the Beatitudes. His inspiration will be amply evident as the reader proceeds through this book. I must thank him also for the time he devoted to reading the final manuscript and for his many excellent suggestions. I am also grateful to fellow faculty members, who never falter in their support and encouragement, particularly Father Richard Byrne, O.C.S.O., Ph.D., our executive director, who also reviewed the book and by his insightful comments facilitated its final production. Thanks are due also to the graduate assistants of the institute, especially Brother Romeo Bonsaint and David Nowak, who aided me in researching several sources, and to our fine and always helpful staff. To all of these members of the institute, as well as to my family and friends in the Domus Dei Corporation, I dedicate this book and ask the Lord to bless them always.

1

Foundations for Living
the Beatitudes

This book is built on the premise that the Beatitudes are foundational attitudes of the spiritual life and that they give form to it as a whole. They are responses to the human aspiration to experience the blessed life, or what St. Catherine of Genoa calls the "instinct for beatitude." [1] They are invitations from a personal God to each of us as persons, calling us to the destiny of peace and joy. These eight attitudes involve all that we have been, all that we are, all that we shall become. They communicate a living expression of the divine direction of each human life.

The Beatitudes preserve the wisdom of the formation tradition, a wisdom we can rely upon in the ebb and flow of changing times. They provide a solid foundation on which to build our life of faith. When we live the Beatitudes in and with the Lord, we become liberated persons in the fullest sense. We follow the path of purgation until, with Jesus, we are filled with the peace of surrender to the Father and led by his Spirit to new depths of intimacy with the Indwelling Trinity. These ways of going to God offer us a truly holistic pattern of formation that involves our entire existence from birth to death and beyond.

Before delving into each of the Beatitudes in turn, we shall consider the importance of formation tradition and its relation to human freedom.

The Dynamism of Tradition

The word *tradition* may at first connote something static or already there, awaiting us in prepackaged fashion. However, any formation tradition is dynamic.[2] The dynamism of tradition points to the many memories that have formed us from earliest childhood and continue to form us in the present and future.[3] It is crucial for us to keep this remembrance of the past alive in the present, for the formation tradition passes on to us a heritage of foundational values as relevant today as they were ages ago. The ways human beings have reached beyond themselves to seek spiritual sustenance have not changed that much. Remembering these transcendent experiences enables us to incorporate their meaning into our present history.

The dynamism of tradition is also sparked by the cumulative memories of our communal or cultural past as a people of God. In Christianity, we could say that our faith is an intertwining of a personal history of redemption with the history of a redeemed people loved deeply by God. To profess this faith is to bear the burden and blessing of all that being chosen means. Our tradition is dynamic in that it takes into account the totality of directives that guide our personal and communal lives. It also draws upon the diverse cultures and peoples in which these formative memories once lived or are still alive today.

Tradition is dynamic in the sense that it involves an ongoing process of selecting and guarding for future generations what is best in the past. Tradition is a repository of values that need to be lived in the present. It teaches us a wisdom we cannot find in books alone. To expose ourselves to it is to risk being changed, for it means reflecting on current times in light of previous generations. We are led inevitably to a wider view of reality than that provided by one lifetime. Perhaps some of our current beliefs will change because of insights gathered from the past. We may hesitate to discard concepts and customs without carefully reflecting on their potential formative meaning.

The Beatitudes, as we shall see, contain such foundational values. The teaching in them, ancient as it is, still challenges us to grow. These are words directed to the heart. To hear them with an open mind is to receive a transmission of values pertinent to human formation. This is so because the Beatitudes expose us to transtemporal wisdom. They evoke reflection and tune into formative human experiences like mourning and persecution that call for a consonant response. If we truly listen to their message, we cannot remain aloof from it. The Beatitudes are thus an excellent example of the dynamism of tradition.

A last consideration pertaining to this dynamism in Christianity has to do with the element, central to our faith, of Incarnation. The fact that God became man profoundly personalizes history. Because the Lord walked on this earth, died, and is with us now in his risen glory, the past is experienced by the Christian as a present and future phenomenon. Christ has died, Christ is risen, Christ will come again. So we pray in the eucharistic acclamation. The Jesus of history is the Risen Lord of the present moment.[4] He is our formative guide. He graces us with a divine destiny. He provides us in the course of time with a providential sense of who we are, of what our life means in its temporal sequence.

The Church is the preserver of tradition insofar as it radiates the presence of the living God in today's world. It orients us as a people by word, liturgy, and sacrament toward the truths Christ lived and died to communicate. It reminds us of the need for self-donating love, for worship and fidelity to the Lord. Through its teachings and living traditions, the Church nourishes our minds and hearts. It helps us to recognize the obstacles that mar our formation journey to God and the conditions that facilitate it.

The dynamism of tradition challenges us to resist absolutizing any one position in the present regardless of what this means in relation to past and future. It encourages us to ponder carefully the mystery of God's will for our life and world. Such a movement into mystery transcends any one generation's information-gathering capacity. It calls for a sound appreciation of tradition, not as a static given, but as a formative guide.

On our side, a dynamic response means that we wrestle with formative directives rather than treat them as abstract concepts to be memorized like historical artifacts. The foundational life directives communicated by a formation tradition must live in our hearts despite the many moments when we may doubt their relevance. In these moments, we need to reflect more deeply upon them in the hope of gaining access to living wisdom.

We could say that tradition at its best forms us as children of God who enjoy the benevolence and freedom of his friendship.

This freedom is not gained automatically. It involves a struggle, a warfare between sin and grace.[5] On the one hand, God calls us to foster foundational life directives that liberate our Christ form. On the other hand, the pride form pulls us back into selfishness and all the ills it breeds.[6] Christ invites us daily to pay attention to the wisdom of the formation tradition and break out of the clutches of formation ignorance.[7] He wants to free us from counterfeit forms of life so that we may experience the liberation of living in our true form and likeness to God.

Our Journey in Freedom

Human freedom is necessarily bound to the reality of who we are as limited creatures. False freedom tries to deny this sense of creatureliness at the base of all religious experience.[8] That is why on our journey to freedom, to the liberation of the children of God, we must take into account the limits and possibilities posed by all levels of formation: pre, intra, inter, and outer.[9] We must carefully appraise directives received from and given to the situation in which we live. Though certain things are preset by that situation, once we accept these limits, we are free to take a creative attitude toward them. Our response is most free when it is congenial with the Christ form of our soul, compatible with the situation in which he has placed us, and compassionate toward our own and others' vulnerability.[10]

Human freedom is this dialogue between situatedness and transcendence. It challenges us to live in the tension between creatureliness and spiritual aspiration. We are invited to go forward, not to regress, to find meaning in situations that may at first glance appear meaningless.[11]

In light of this tension between limits and transcendence, two avenues seem open to human beings. One would be to look at these limits and despair; the other would be to reflect upon possibilities inherent in them and turn toward hope. Those who see only limits feel lost in a senseless universe. They live a despondent life-style. Those who see limits as possibilities to go beyond live a hopeful life-style. People who give up and exist from day to day in quiet desperation do not exercise their freedom.[12] True freedom is found in people who maintain what the philosopher Paul Ricoeur calls the "passion for the possible." [13]

Such persons live their freedom in the light of hope. In spite of the darkness of sin, despair, inhumanity, and persecution, they experience the "how much more" of God's promise of redemption. To live in freedom (and hence to live the Beatitudes) means to assess the formative potential in such seemingly negative experiences as suffering and death. Despite the negativity of the Cross, the disciples are free to hope in the face of what appears to be impossible. Their passion for the possible enables them to validate the Resurrection. By living in the light of hope, they are able to glimpse the fullness of peace and joy awaiting them.

This passion for the possible is exemplified in Jesus, who in spite of cruelty chose to be kind, who in spite of injustice responded with mercy. The Beatitudes he teaches presume a response in freedom to this "how much more" of faith. They assure us that in the face of sorrow, hunger and thirst, and persecution, we are capable of following the way of compassion and peace. Out of limitation, prejudice, and pain comes the passion for the possible. Such is the Christian understanding of our journey into freedom. Through faith in the "how much more" of God's love, we are strengthened to overcome the obstacles of pride and discouragement. We are able to love others as we are loved by God.

Hope, in the words of Ricoeur, has a "fissuring power." [14] It breaks into the misery of sin and reminds us of the mercy of God. It breaks through the expectations we might have of how God would respond. It enables us to hope in his unpredictable generosity toward humanity. Hope, in other words, dislocates our human expectations and enables us to look upon life from a divine perspective. It makes possible the recovery of formative meaning. That meaning is always there, but our vision is blocked by pride and human concerns. We need the fissuring power of hope to see anew the goodness, mercy, and care of God for man, to see his hand guiding past, present, and future.

The past no longer appears as a haphazard collection of events. It falls into a meaningful pattern. Trusting in the forming presence of God, we can humbly appraise his will and, if necessary, reset our priorities. We strive to be more faithful than ever to the truths of the formation tradition, rooted in the Scriptures, validated by the experiences of generations of Christians, and witnessed to in the writings of the spiritual masters.

Now we can listen anew to the message of the Beatitudes. They become a "deposit of evaluation," a restful oasis in the changing course of man's history.[15] We can trust that the life directives illumined in them are formative and that they must be lived generation after generation. These directives foster human freedom because they offer food for reflection. They respect the slow maturation process that characterizes human formation. As manifestations of God's blessings, they carry the living spirit of his new law.

The Beatitudes thus bless the human condition, which, though limited, is full of promise in the eyes of the Lord. These blessings affirm our deepest aspirations for goodness, freedom, harmony, and wholeness. In the Beatitudes, Transcendent Mystery meets finite limits and offers us the possibility of union and communion. The Lord invites us to let go of our legalistic fears and to flow with who we most truly are. He invites us to release the Christ form of our soul and to experience the grace of eternal beatitude.

Notes

1. *"When a soul is close to its first creation,*
      pure and unstained,
    the instinct for beatitude asserts itself
      with such impetus and fiery charity
    that any impediment becomes unbearable."

St. Catherine of Genoa, *Purgation and Purgatory: The Classics of Western Spirituality* (New York: Paulist Press, 1979), p. 73.

2. See Noel Dermott O'Donoghue, "The Dynamism of Tradition," in *Heaven in Ordinarie* (Springfield, Ill.: Templegate, 1979), pp. 122–35; and Christopher Bryant, *The Heart in Pilgrimage: Christian Guidelines for the Human Journey* (New York: The Seabury Press, 1980).

3. Formatively understood, memory pertains to "the residues in human life of past formation and deformation that potentially or actually still influence the present direction and formation of that life. . . ." See Adrian van Kaam, "Formative Memory," *Studies in Formative Spirituality* 2 (1981): 117.

4. See Karl Rahner, "Jesus Christ," in *Foundations of Christian Faith* (New York: The Seabury Press, 1978), pt. VI, pp. 176–321.

5. "Our only hope of human and spiritual survival lies in a victory which must take place first in our own hearts and then extend its influence to those of others." See Aelred Squire, "Holy Warfare," in *Asking the Fathers: The Art of Meditation and Prayer* (New York: Paulist Press, 1973), ch. 9, pp. 100–101.

6. Ills bred by the pride form are discussed at length by St. Catherine of Siena in *The Dialogue: The Classics of Western Spirituality* (New York: Paulist Press, 1980). See especially pp. 251–55.

7. "Formation ignorance is an ignorance of the true transcendent nature of formation, an ignorance common to people since the Fall." See Adrian van Kaam, "Formation Ignorance," *G, Studies* 1 (1980): 458.

8. For a discussion of false freedom and the denial of creatureliness, see Baron Friedrich von Hügel, *The Mystical Element of Religion as Studied in Saint Catherine of Genoa and Her Friends,* vol. 1 (London: James Clarke & Co., 1961).

9. See Adrian van Kaam's references to "Infra-Formation" and "Intra-Formation" in *G, Studies* 1 (1980): 137–38.

10. "The means to attain the fully consonant life form is the progressively congenial, compatible, and compassionate exercise of formative mind, will, and the other formation powers in increasing mutual harmony." See Adrian van Kaam, "Means to Attainment of the Fully Consonant Life Form," *G, Studies* 1 (1980): 464.

11. Two extraordinary testimonies to the power of finding meaning in debilitating human circumstances—Russian and German concentration camps—can be discovered in the transcendent accounts of Walter J. Ciszek, S.J., *He Leadeth Me* (Garden City, N.Y.: Doubleday & Co., Image Books, 1973); and Viktor E. Frankl, *Man's Search for Meaning* (New York: Simon & Schuster, Pocket Books, 1963).

12. That the mass of men lead lives of quiet desperation is the conclusion of Henry David Thoreau in *Walden and Civil Disobedience* (Boston: Houghton-Mifflin Co., Riverside Editions, 1957).

13. See Paul Ricoeur, "Metaphor and the Main Problem of Hermeneutics," in *The Philosophy of Paul Ricoeur: An Anthology of His Work,* ed. Charles E. Reagan and David Stewart (Boston: Beacon Press, 1978), pp. 134–48 and 32–35.

14. Ricoeur, "The Hermeneutics of Symbols," in ibid., p. 57. See also Jacques Ellul, *Hope in Time of Abandonment* (New York: The Seabury Press, 1977).

15. Ricoeur, "Existence and Hermeneutics," in *The Philosophy of Paul Ricoeur,* pp. 97–108.

2

Formative Reading and Living of the Beatitudes

From the perspective of foundational formation, the Beatitudes are calls to holiness and guidelines for our journey toward the freedom of the children of God. They are attitudes of being directed less to external actions and more toward the inner life of transformation, toward the heart. Out of this graced transformation comes the strength and courage to offer Christian witness wherever we are. The Beatitudes express formative directives that lead to the unfolding of Christ-like dispositions. Taken together, they lay out a plan of life affecting our inner being and the world in which we live.

The Beatitudes call us to a way of being that is the opposite of what we might expect in a worldly sense. Happiness does not mean amassing possessions, but being poor in spirit. Rather than dominating others to feel important, we are to be gentle and full of mercy. Instead of running away from suffering, we are to welcome persecution for holiness' sake.

Read in the context of the Lord's life, these sayings are at once inspirational and incarnational. They invite us to realize our fullest potential for transcendence as well as to exercise our capacity to form and reform our situation and world. At first glance, what appear to be passive attitudes become in the Beatitudes the highest forms of human freedom and activity. For instance, in his blessing of the lowly, Jesus challenges us to answer provocation not with irritation but with gentle concern. He asks us to let go of the claims of worldly honor and live in the humility that God will exalt.

The impact of this message can only be appreciated over a lifetime of reading, rereading, and, most of all, living these foundational truths. If we engage seriously in such formative reading and reflection, it can have a transforming effect. Taking these directives to heart implies trying to incarnate their wisdom day by day. Therefore, before proceeding to a more in-depth consideration of the Purgative, Illuminative, and Unitive Beatitudes, let us reflect in general on all the Beatitudes as inspirational dynamics from which Christ-like actions flow.

Purgation as Mourning and Sorrow

The experience of mourning serves as a blessed reminder that we are called by Christ to relinquish our fascination with what is transitory. Any time we absolutize the temporal as if it were eternal, we live in self-deception. The sword of sorrow frees us from this deceptive posture. Sadness grips us when we have to admit that all is ultimately passing. Thus this Beatitude helps us to appraise what is truly lasting and to find our consolation there. Accepting the pain of finitude purifies us of illusions of earthly immortality and prepares us to enter the bliss of eternity. The grief incurred when expectations are crushed is unsettling, but this kind of sadness can free us for a new depth of intimacy with the Divine.

Purgation as a Hungering for Holiness

On this formation journey, God summons us time and again to pursue holiness, no matter what the cost to our comfort. This hunger for holiness cannot be satisfied by the physical food of success in this world. "Not on bread alone is man to live but on every utterance that comes from the mouth of God" (Mt. 4:4). We suffer knowing that this God-directed desire can only be fulfilled in the life to come. Yet this suffering is a great grace because it enables us to commit our lives more fully to the love and service of God, from which no human imperfection can separate us. His grace works sufficiently in our weakness (2 Cor. 13:4).

Purgation as Persecution

Others who have resisted God's call or refused his grace may openly or covertly persecute us through expressions of envy, ridicule, misunderstanding; outright violence, even torture, may be the result of our trying to live in the truth of Christ. These are harsh crosses to bear, but such persecution is unavoidable if we are his followers. Freedom can only be ours when we renounce our fear of suffering and accept persecution for holiness' sake. The Lord had to suffer reproach and humiliation, even from those who professed to be his friends. We must not be surprised if the same happens to us in overt or subtle ways, yet, like him, we must not lose sight of the goal of our journey: the reign of God.

Illumination in Mercy

In the midst of our suffering, we encounter the tender compassion of the Lord. In and through him, we are to show mercy to all those who become our traveling companions on the way of transformation. When we behold in compassion the vulnerability of others, we radiate something of God's love for all members of his family.

Illumination in Lowliness

A mark of discipleship is our desire to remain docile, Christ-formed creatures even under the most difficult circumstances. We are able to do so only if we have experienced that we do not have to carry our burdens alone. Grace strengthens us to transcend human insufficiency. Meekly, we can perceive how worthless we are without the Lord. This perception severs the tentacles of pride; it unlocks the prison of mere self-reliance and releases in us the joy Mary felt when she proclaimed:

> . . . *my spirit finds joy in God my savior,*
> *For he has looked upon his servant in her lowliness;*
> *all ages to come shall call me blessed.*
>
> (Lk. 1:47–48)

Illumination in Peacemaking

As the peace of the Lord pervades our being, anger and hostility, bitterness and revenge—these and other negative attitudes are gradually left behind like so much excess baggage. The lighter the load, the faster we can travel to our destination. For our goal is to reach God. Since he has given us the gift of his own peace (Jn. 14:27), we must put aside warring factionalism within ourselves or between ourselves and others. There is no place for such divisiveness when one is journeying to God.

Unity through Poverty of Spirit

The spirit of poverty draws us into intimacy with God. It is the antithesis of the spirit of pride that tears us from him. To live in poverty is to acknowledge who we are as creatures, depending on him for our life and being. Poverty of spirit becomes our way of identifying with Christ's self-emptying love for humankind. Because of this spirit, God can draw us into the household of the Trinity whereas, without humility, we risk forfeiting our entrance to the reign of God.

Unity through Purity of Heart

In our hearts, we intend to surrender to God's will and to resist whatever we discover as contrary to his calling. This purity of intention, this attempt to be truly single-hearted, is a sign of our graced unity with him. The more our hearts seek God alone, the stronger his love inflames our being and consumes the last traces of pride. This flame burns away whatever separates us from the love of God, leaving us freer to live in his light and to release the Christ form, the core of our being. In this light, we become who he intends us to be. We behold at long last where our journey is leading us.

From this overview of the Beatitudes, we can see that each of them, to use van Kaam's term, is a kind of symbolic pointer to the kingdom of God every human being is called to inherit.[1] Living these attitudes opens us to the life of formative benediction all persons seek.[2] Reading them prayerfully, we gain insight into what it means to be a new creation, transformed by Christ and free to respond to divine directives that lead to union with the Father. For beyond the immediate significance of these texts is the mystery of transforming union our souls long to reach.

Mourning, meekness, poverty of spirit—all seem to describe a condition of being acted upon, and yet, looked at from a transcendent perspective, they are dynamic invitations to be and become in a whole new way—in this case, to experience consolation, to inherit the earth, to enter God's kingdom. What appear to be passive attitudes to the functional ego point to a new kind of activity on the level of the spirit. They free us to be present to Christ in a unique way while fully participating in service to the Christian community.

As readers in need of formative direction, we cannot remain at a distance from these words. We must enter into their many levels of meaning while trying to embody their implications for personal and social living. Reading the Beatitudes thus becomes an exercise in reading one's own life. This is so because they are rooted in the main dynamic of human and Christian formation: our transcendent aspiration for life and meaning beyond the functional and vital limits of each human situation.[3]

Those times of purification, when our pride is broken, may lead to a new or renewed faith commitment. This marks a turning point. Rather than falling into despondency, we acknowledge our need for God. Confidence in him can occasion a shift from feeling broken to a sense of breaking through to a depth of encounter with One who has never ceased to care for us. This inner illumination prepares us for those moments when God may take the initiative and grant us the grace of transforming union.[4]

Notes

1. See Adrian van Kaam, "The Hypothesis of Symbolic Pointers," *Studies in Formative Spirituality* 2 (1981): 523–24.

2. See Adrian van Kaam, "Formative Benediction," *G, Studies* 1 (1980): 146.

3. "The central dynamic or spark of human formation is the transconscious aspiration after the fulfilling life form." Adrian van Kaam. "Main Dynamic Sources of Human Formation," *G, Studies* 1 (1980): 297.

4. See Adrian van Kaam, "Consonance and Transforming Union," *G, Studies* 2 (1981): 510.

THE
PURGATIVE
BEATITUDES

3

Blessed Are Those Who Mourn, for They Shall Be Comforted

My soul weeps for sorrow;
strengthen me according to your words.
Ps. 119: 28

Those that sow in tears
shall reap rejoicing.
Although they go forth weeping,
carrying the seed to be sown,
They shall come back rejoicing,
carrying their sheaves.
Ps 126: 5–6

Introduction

In each of the Beatitudes, there are two interlocked dimensions: proclamation and promise. In the proclamation, the first part of the blessing, something is declared about the being of the person. This points to the foundational reality that will form the basis of our consideration of the Beatitude in relation to human presence. Each Beatitude also contains, in the second part, a promise. Thus something is said about the person, and then something of what will be is foretold.

The movement from proclamation to promise requires an act of faith, for embedded in each Beatitude is a kind of paradox from the point of view of human understanding. We can identify with what is proclaimed about who we are. Indeed, we are people who feel sorrow. We understand this experience because of the limits of the human condition. What strikes us as paradoxical is the fact that the Lord blesses us in our sorrow. We ask logically how can sorrow be a blessing? To proceed from this proclamation to the promise of consolation truly demands a "venture of faith." [1]

Thus the Beatitudes pertain not only to the here-and-now condition in which we find ourselves but also to the future in formative anticipation of what can be, if our faith is firm enough. [2] These texts intend to articulate essential conditions for fully human and Christian living. That is what makes their message so powerful. As attitudes, they are relevant to human presence as such, as well as to the nature of persons as openness to the transcendent. This openness may remain implicit or it can become explicit through allegiance to a Sacred Other, a system of beliefs, and, in the case of Christianity, to a definitive revelation of God to humanity. Only to the degree that we are growing in faith can we hear the proclamation of each blessing and experience in this life, and surely in the life to come, its promise.

Sorrow and Mourning: The Human Foundation

Our experience of everyday life enables us to identify with the sense of sorrow proclaimed in this Beatitude. Certainly we mourn when we lose a friend or family member. Any serious loss is a form of personal deprivation. [3]

I remember how terrible I felt when my maternal grandmother died. Though I was only nine at the time, I had my first taste of the tragic separation death brings. Later I understood that this distance, so irreversible from the human viewpoint, awakens in the heart of the mourner a strange sense of nearness.

I would never see her laughing eyes light up again. I would never hear her infectious laughter or touch the crinkly skin on her cheek or smell the freshly-baked-bread odor of her lithe body. Someone precious had gone out of my life. An indescribable, aching emptiness was left where once the warmest person had been. It seemed as if the emptiness would never pass . . . yet it did. Time healed the wound of her absence, and with that healing came a new awareness of her presence. [4] The physical person was dead, but her spirit was more alive than ever.

The sorrow, which initially seemed to draw our relationship to a close, was actually the avenue that opened me to the greatest consolation. In some way, she became nearer to me in death than she had been in life. Spiritually she would never leave me. All she stood for would become a part of my being—her humility and humor, her dedication and endurance. The many personal and spiritual values she lived could be carried on in the members of her family.

Mourning, which at first glance appears to be only passive, can be a blessed event if we see it in the context of formative remembrance.[5] The experience of sorrow helps us to remember our finitude. Often we press death into the background of our thoughts because we are afraid to face it. We try to escape its finality, but the loss of someone we love makes us think. In our grief, we remember not only the other but ourselves as well.

This remembrance of who we are can be the beginning of a saving experience. When we remember that everything is passing, that all persons, things, and events as we know them shall one day disappear, the pathos of reality itself draws us to meditation. We are less inclined to take life for granted, to fall into complacency. We become more awake, aware, and appreciative. Each day is a gift to be lived simply.

Formative remembrance influences intra- as well as interformation. It helps to dislodge the attachments that bind us to anyone or anything as ultimate. Formative detachment enables us to accept our limits and to appraise situations more realistically.[6] In this light, it is possible to grow more gentle toward ourselves and all who are wounded and in need of consolation.

Such detachment not only heightens our perception of passing beauty; it also reminds us that the aim of our longing transcends any earthly particular. In this action of detachment, we cease clinging to what was or is and turn toward the hope of what is to come. Daily dying may take the form of our becoming less rushed and more patient, less aggressive and more tender. We can start to love ourselves and others in a new way.

In this turning, we begin to see the emergence of a religious horizon. Sorrow as a human experience shatters the illusion of self-sufficiency. It breaks through the deception that we are in control of our life. We can no longer cover over our contingency with efficiency, functionalism, and the amassing of possessions. Sorrow reminds us of our weakness. It disrupts our secure world and compels us to look beyond the illusion of control to the Divine Source of comfort.

Sorrow and Transcendence: The Religious Articulation

Mourning is a mode of purgation. Purgation thrusts us into sorrow. Such suffering could evoke despair were it not for the possibility that there is something more. Purgation lights up our potential for transcendence. It invites us to explore the experiences that accompany mourning and sorrow—consolations that can occur when we least expect them.

On a summer night, walking under the stars, I may feel suddenly uplifted by their beauty. Though the day has been filled with small moments of sadness, these pale in importance compared to the vastness of the cosmos. I feel sustained by One who holds this universe in harmonious order. These stars, like life itself, burn brightly, then fade, but the Sacred lasts forever.

This brief beholding is a gifted moment that cannot be sustained. It is followed by my return, with some sadness, to everyday life. The sadness is there because I have beheld, however briefly, the Source of life, a presence that evokes longing and loneliness. I know my spirit is destined for eventual union with this Other, even though I have experienced that presence for only a short duration.

Despite such gifted moments, the impact of the everyday tends to repress awareness of the Transcendent. Forgetfulness may take the form of inertia, protective security measures, the desire to maintain the status quo. We build elaborate systems of defense to ward off the awareness that we are dying daily.[7] Yet it is clear that these defenses make no difference in the end. Each time the sense of contingency surfaces, we feel anxious. But instead of facing our concern and questioning that toward which it points, we cover it over with more efficiency. As long as all goes well and we remain in a dominant position, we feel little or no inclination to deal with the deep discontent connected with consciousness of our own ultimate death—the same consciousness that convinces us that there must be more than this.

What happens when we come face to face with a limit experience like illness? Suddenly our security is shattered by sorrow. We are in acute discomfort. Pain disrupts our control. We cannot heal our bodies at will. Agony reveals the relativity of former signs of happiness like wealth and success. What do these things mean to a severely ill or dying person? Here the "haves" and "have-nots" are equal. One knows what it is to be without defenses, alone and dependent.

Grief can become an opportunity not to despise our helplessness but to seek consolation. It is all right to be vulnerable, to wonder if we are merely the victim of uncaring forces. Faith is tested by mourning. Is the Sacred a caring power, desirous of fostering through the experience of mourning our formation as spiritual beings? To be snapped out of forgetfulness by suffering is not an act of vengeance but of grace. Our tears flow into the ocean of Divine Goodness, and we are carried beyond sorrow to consolation.

Thus we see two ways to respond to the experience of mourning as religious persons. One response involves a regressive movement into dejection and discouragement. This is the "sickness of mourning." Feelings of being treated unjustly come to the fore. We cannot accept the given and work from there. We fall into despondency. A more formative option is the "response of remembrance." This signifies the progressive movement of purgative mourning. We remember who we are, accept the current reality, and respond to it creatively. This formative response helps us to overcome any resentment we may feel toward the Sacred as the cause of our troubles. Neither blame nor bargaining can help us. The challenge is to live in the hope that some good will come out of this situation. All we can do now is wait. The time of weeping will pass, and even if it does not, we can gain comfort from the fact that we are facing reality and not a false world of our own making.

Now we may be ready to receive the promise of this Beatitude. Sorrow is blessed because through it we may be able to sense who we are and why we must reach beyond ourselves to God. Only from him, in some mysterious way, can we receive the comfort that refreshes our inmost being. He gives us the strength to face our finitude; to look death in the eye and not feel its sting; to accept pain in our lives as an invitation to disclose new directive meanings. Sorrow beseeches us to return to God, whereas in our security we tend to forget him entirely. Purgation as mourning reminds us that on our journey God may refresh us at wayside places, but we must not mistake these for home. If we seek the depth dimension of what we are experiencing, we shall find the comfort and consolation offered by our Savior.

Consolation in Christ: The Christian Articulation

When we look at life from a Christian perspective, we learn that experiences that seem useless humanly are the occasions Christ uses to draw us into new appraisals. This applies to death, which shall be consoled. Purgation has a place in God's plan in that it gives us a chance to seek healing, if not of body, then of soul.

Mourning opens us to being comforted by God. He takes our suffering and turns it into joy, provided we let go of ego-centered despondency and open ourselves to participation in the Cross. Only by passing through death can we enjoy new life. Such purgation is not a sign of defeat but a move forward in life direction. It offers us an opportunity to follow Jesus in that surrender through which one attains true glory. He promises us that though we weep and mourn for a time while the world rejoices, our grief will be turned into joy—a joy no one can take from us (Jn. 16: 20–22).

When our inner resources dry up, when we are incapable of doing anything about what is happening to us, when all else seems lost, faith in God's promise remains to sustain us.[8] In our cry for help, there is both desperation and hope. We are sad now, but this experience readies us for a bliss that shall be unending, when God himself will gather us into his arms and wipe away our tears (Rev. 7:15–17).

Jesus' promise of consolation points simultaneously in two directions—present and future. Many times, comfort comes at the moment we need it. God does not test us beyond what we can endure. He hears our prayers and takes pity on us. His promise is also eschatological. It assures us that we are in a waiting period leading to a glory yet to be revealed. We believe with St. Paul that what we suffer in this life can never be compared to the glory that awaits us (Rm. 8:18–19). During this waiting time, the Holy Spirit will be our advocate. When we are so overcome by sorrow that we cannot find words to pray, he expresses our plea. He knows what we feel and what we need. Hence we can be confident now since our reward then is so great (Heb. 10:32).

According to van Kaam, this anticipation is formative because it fosters transcendent appraisal of what is happening to us here and now.[9] If we can pass through the purgation of mourning, we shall enjoy the fullness of God's presence. Our task, in cooperation with grace, is to seek the meaning of these events. Often, sorrow strikes us in the form of repentance. We feel wretched because of our sin. We long for reconciliation with God while wondering what happened to our good intentions. We weep for what we have done in comparison to what we could have been, had we obeyed.

Such sorrow hastens our return to God if we have faith in his forgiveness. This explains again why Jesus blesses those who mourn, especially when they mourn for their loss of likeness to him and their foolish seeking after worldly fulfillment. Spiritual masters compare this thirst of the soul to parched land. Sin makes one feel dull of mind and devoid of the power to penetrate the profound truths of God. Repentance restores faith and the feeling of how much more there is to come. Our tireless expectancy in the midst of mourning prompts his forgiveness. It leads us to see that only in God can our souls find rest (Ps. 62). He alone can heal our woundedness by redeeming grace.

The more we turn to him, the more we experience the consolation promised in this Beatitude. We forget the past and press on to what lies ahead, trusting that in this life, and surely in the next, he will purify us of all traces of sin and make us worthy to enjoy his presence eternally. This confidence in God strengthens us more than anything else. We know there will come a time of peace and repose that will be of eternal duration. Thus our deep interior sorrow due to sin can itself be seen as a sign of his grace.

The author of *The Cloud of Unknowing* goes so far as to advise his disciple to plunge himself into this experience of perfect sorrow so that he can realize not only who he is, a child of God, but that he is a being made in God's image and likeness. This heartfelt repentance purifies the soul of sin and even of the inclination to sin. Deep interior sorrow arises from the naked knowing and feeling of our own being.[10] Though we may try to rid ourselves of this feeling, it persists as a graced reminder of our dependence on God. The author's words merit quoting here:

> You must be careful never to strain your body or spirit irreverently. Simply sit relaxed and quiet but plunged and immersed in sorrow. The sorrow I speak of is genuine and perfect, and blessed is the man who experiences it. Every man has plenty of cause for sorrow but he alone understands the deep universal reason for sorrow who experiences *that he is.* Every motive pales beside this one. He alone feels authentic sorrow who realizes not only *what he is* but *that he is.* Anyone who has not felt this should really weep, for he has never experienced real sorrow. This sorrow purifies a man of sin and sin's punishment. Even more, it prepares his heart to receive that joy through which he will finally transcend the knowing and feeling of his being.[11]

The person who feels such compunction of heart can move from this sorrow to "reverent longing for God's salvation, for otherwise no human being could sustain it."[12] Prayer flows from compunction. Without such contact with the Sacred, we might end up despising ourselves and feeling forsaken. With it, feelings of desperation can turn into aspirations for transcendence.

St. John of the Cross offers a similar understanding in his "Spiritual Canticle." He reflects that it is the absence of the Beloved that causes continual moaning in the lover.[13] The soul can only moan in sorrow because it has been touched by God. It has been wounded by love and now mourns because no medicine can be found to heal these wounds of love, save the presence of the One who caused them. Thus the soul becomes detached from all that is not God. She surrenders to him and anticipates his surrender to her. Her interior suffering may at times be unspeakable, but immense good will come of it.

The soul's motivation for repentance goes deeper than merely making restitution for past sins. The soul laments her loss of a sense of wholeness and hence consonance with the will of God, who is All in all. This graced experience of oneness is the sought-for consolation of the sufferer.

In "The Living Flame of Love," St. John counsels the soul to accept these "delectable or delightful wounds" from God's hands as a good remedy for forgetfulness and sin.[14] These wounds root out the pride form and enable us, by embracing the Cross, to live more consciously in his presence. As St. John puts it in his "Sayings of Light and Love," "In tribulation, immediately draw near to God with confidence, and you will receive strength, enlightenment, and instruction."[15] He adds in his "Maxims and Counsels," "Love consists not in feeling great things but in having great detachment and in suffering for the Beloved."[16]

Like all purgative experiences, mourning and sorrow cleanse us of false expectations and the formation dissonance bred by thoughtless absorption in cultural pulsations. These experiences remind us of our need to remain open to the whole, consonant picture of transcendent formation.[17] From the Christian perspective, such occasions of suffering assure us that only by embracing the Cross can we find comfort and new reasons for living. Submission to God's will enables us to turn from subjectivistic mediocrity to creative adherence to the whole formation mystery. We place our narrow views pertaining to the meaning of life against the horizon of all that is. From this perspective, sorrow becomes a window through which we can see the whole and the Holy.

Practical Applications of This Beatitude in Ongoing Formation

In the science of formative spirituality, we try to apply these principles of living to concrete practices. This means that we need to recognize obstacles that hinder these attitudes of being so that we can try to create conditions that facilitate their unfolding. Not only must we know the formative potential of living the Beatitudes in theory, but we must also practice this way of living concretely.

Obstacles

What happens if our only response to mourning and sorrow is gloom and pessimism, or dejection and depression? Depression can be an obstacle to formation, depending on whether it is reactive or endogenous.[18] *Reactive depression* refers to the normal reaction we feel to loss of any kind—for instance, the loss of a person we loved, of a position we craved, of a promotion we deserved. Reactive depression is also related to the many sorrows we feel from any kind of separation. It has an identifiable object toward which and because of which we feel depressed. Working these feelings through can foster spiritual formation.

Endogenous depression is a more serious problem because here the source of sadness or anguish seems to reside within us and we cannot shake ourselves loose from it. Neither can it be explained reasonably by external circumstances—they do not seem so objectively horrific as to have caused such a response. In other words, endogenous depression extends in time and depth beyond normal expectations. It can become a severe problem if we do not work it through, preferably with the help of a physician or counselor. In the throes of endogenous depression, we may forsake faith and lose all hope. Thus it poses a severe obstacle to formation.

Another obstacle related to this Beatitude is excessive self-pity in the face of sorrow, which may, in turn, be grounded in introspectionism and the loss of the capacity to meditate reflectively. Perfectionism is another problem.[19] Anything that diminishes one's exalted self-image may evoke an inexplicable sorrow. When one needs to be perfect, one is incapable of admitting weakness. When things go wrong, one blames oneself and is unable to receive needed consolation. One feels unworthy of being comforted and falls into a depressed state.

Such chronic brooding often leads to decreased effectiveness, pervasive fatigue, even hypochondria and consequent psychosomatic symptoms that may be stress-related.[20] Because one begins to believe that nothing matters, one pays less and less attention to one's work. Stress doubles because one still has to produce. Repressing feelings of rage only makes things worse. To keep one's system of excessive security directives going requires such an outlay of energy that one never feels rested. Small sicknesses may be blown into major maladies. One is likely, in fact, to get more infectious diseases because the vital and transcendent dimensions of one's life are so weakened.

Steady loss of productivity, combined with chronic tiredness and a repertoire of excuses for not doing one's work, result in an irritable, somber temperament. An eyebrow raised in criticism makes such people crouch in self-pity or flare up in anger. Noticeable as well may be a growing tendency toward withdrawal. They begin to separate themselves from friends who want to help. They do not trust their own good intentions and may project onto them the hatred they feel for themselves. They may become somewhat paranoid, feeling that people are talking about them and that their problems are the center of others' attention. They convince themselves that no one could understand what they are going through, so they bottle up their frustration. They feel martyred by the pain they have to undergo, while at the same time they believe that they are so bad they deserve this punishment.

The causes of these conditions are manifold and must be dealt with by someone engaged in the work of psychological and spiritual formation. It takes great skill and patience to work with such persons because, at least in the beginning, they need to keep their life under rigid control. If one peg crumbles, they fear that the whole edifice of their carefully erected scheme of life will collapse. The question that concerns us is: Can people grow through this self-negating state to the point where they can hear again the call of this Beatitude, assuring them that sorrow is a blessing and that God seeks through it to grant them the grace of consolation? A lot depends on their willingness to gain insight into their anxious, angry, depressed condition. Help may be possible only through good medical treatment, therapy, and supportive formative direction.[21] In addition to these aids, there are certain conditions that facilitate this transition from sorrow to consolation.

Conditions

First of all, one needs to move from self-pity to self-knowledge in the deepest sense. Pity is often a manifestation of hidden pride. *I* feel sorry for *myself* because *I* want things to go *my* way and they never do. Self-knowledge is really another word for humility. It means, according to St. Teresa of Avila, that we walk in the truth of who we are.[22] We acknowledge that Christ is the foundational form of our being. We understand the depth of our dependence on him. Despite sin, he has found us worthy of love and lasting consolation.

Second, both with ourselves and others, we try to avoid exaggerating our sorrows, worries, anxieties, and troubles. The twin practices of meditation and moderation are advisable here. If we can place our problems against the wide horizon of transcendence, their intensity will be diffuse. This faith vision, perhaps enhanced by a sense of humor, helps us to avoid despondency and to await patiently the lifting of this shadow of sorrow by the Lord. It is better to wait upon him than to force consolation. We trust he is sending suffering for a reason, and thus we modify our expectations of comfort. In desolation or consolation, our love does not change.[23]

A third facilitating condition is perseverance. We must be determined, as St. Teresa says, with a strong determination always to obey God's will and to accept the grace of purgation in whatever form it comes.[24] Such perserverance helps us to move from concentration on our sorrow toward loving longing for God. Feelings of desperation become reminders of transcendence and the need to trust more. Compunction of heart increases our courage to detach ourselves from selfish motivations and center our lives in Christ.

It also helps if we can see our mourning as part of humanity's experience. Who among us does not suffer some sorrow throughout life? Who among us does not have occasion to weep? God sends these gifts of mourning and sorrow into our lives so we can experience the grace of purgation already on earth and thus foster our "instinct for beatitude."[25] He gives us this chance to weep now so we can laugh later (Lk. 6:21). By contrast, he warns those who laugh now that they may be sorry later, for what does it profit a man to gain the whole world and to lose himself in the process? (Mt. 16:26). We are thus grateful to God for the times of mourning he sends into our lives. He challenges us to treat them not as obstacles but as graced opportunities to purge our hearts of egoism so that we may grow transparent with love of him.

In this light, we can truly say that our mourning has been turned into joy. We are able to give up our old complacent life form and welcome the new form Christ has enabled us to become. As we grow closer to God, we sense even in suffering his ceaseless consolation. At once we see and experience the basic truth of this Beatitude, We mourn because we have forgotten the simple sense of God's allness. Sorrow rightly overtakes us. For all our cleverness, we are farther away from happiness than ever.

Mourning now becomes a blessed opportunity for being called back. We must return in formative reading and living, in meditation and prayer, to the deepest source of our life, to the timeless truth that God is near. All our losses and failures have been blessings in disguise, benevolent messengers reminding us that only in him shall we find consolation that lasts, that only in him shall we live and laugh again.

Notes

1. Søren Kierkegaard, as quoted in Hans Küng, *Does God Exist? An Answer for Today,* trans. Edward Quinn (Garden City, N.Y.: Doubleday & Co., 1980), pp. 71–73.

2. Adrian van Kaam, "Formative Anticipation," *Studies in Formative Spirituality* 2 (1981): 120.

3. See Adrian van Kaam, "Structural Deprivation," *G, Studies* 1 (1980): 150.

4. See C. S. Lewis, *A Grief Observed* (New York: Bantam Books, 1976); and Sheldon Vanauken, *A Severe Mercy,* Davy's edition (New York: Harper & Row, 1980).

5. Adrian van Kaam, "Formative Remembrance," *G, Studies* 2 (1981): 118.

6. Adrian van Kaam, "Formative Detachment," *G, Studies* 1 (1980): 151.

7. See Ernest Becker, *The Denial of Death* (New York: The Free Press, 1973), ch. 2, pp. 11–24.

8. In *Brokenness* (Cincinnati: St. Anthony Messenger Press, 1980), six women share their sorrows and struggles for acceptance and peace, wisdom, and faith.

9. Adrian van Kaam, "Global Appraisal Formation Sources," *G, Studies* 1 (1980): 43.

10. This reference to the naked intent toward God in the depths of our being is found in *The Cloud of Unknowing,* ed. William Johnston (Garden City, N.Y.: Doubleday & Co., Image Books, 1973), pp. 48–49.

11. Ibid., p. 103.

12. Ibid., p. 104.

13. St. John of the Cross, "The Spiritual Canticle," in *The Collected Works of St. John of the Cross,* trans. Kieran Kavanaugh, O.C.D, and Otilio Rodriguez, O.C.D (Washington, D.C.: Institute of Carmelite Studies, ICS Publications, 1973), pp. 421–22.

14. Ibid., "The Living Flame of Love," pp. 597–600.

15. Ibid., "Sayings of Light and Love," p. 672.

16. Ibid., "Maxims and Counsels," *Maxims on Love,* p. 676.

17. For insight into the consonance of formation versus dissonance, see Adrian

van Kaam, "Consonance Aspiration," *G, Studies* 2 (1981): 509; and "Deformative Results of Binding of the Formation Power," *G, Studies* 1 (1980): 229.

18. For an interesting discussion of depression as an obstacle to formation, see Nathan S. Kline, M.D., *From Sad to Glad* (New York: Ballantine Books, 1974).

19. For reflections on perfectionism and excessive security drives, see Adrian van Kaam, *In Search of Spiritual Identity* (Denville, N.J.: Dimension Books, 1975), ch. 6, pp. 161 and 166–67, and ch. 7, pp. 172–96. See also Adrian van Kaam, "Perfectionistic Deformation of Christian Life Formation," *G, Studies* 2 (1981): 500; "Perfectionism and the Demonic," *G, Studies* 2 (1981): 523; and "Security Directives," *G, Studies* 2 (1981): 534.

20. See Hans Seyle, M.D., *The Stress of Life* (New York: McGraw-Hill Book Co., 1976); Meyer Friedman and Ray H. Rosenman, *Type A Behavior and Your Heart* (Greenwich, Conn.: Fawcett Crest Book, 1974); and Edmund Jacobson, *You Must Relax* (New York: McGraw-Hill Book Co., 1962).

21. See Carolyn Gratton, *Guidelines for Spiritual Direction: Studies in Formative Spirituality*, vol. 3 (Denville, N.J.: Dimension Books, 1980).

22. St. Teresa of Avila, "Interior Castle," in *The Collected Works of St. Teresa of Avila*, vol. 2, trans. Kieran Kavanaugh, O.C.D. and Otilio Rodriguez, O.C.D. (Washington, D.C.: Institute of Carmelite Studies, ICS Publications, 1980), p. 420.

23. See St. Francis de Sales, *Introduction to the Devout Life* (Garden City, N.Y.: Doubleday & Co., Image Books, 1966); Susan Muto, *Steps Along the Way: The Path of Spiritual Reading* (Denville, N.J.: Dimension Books, 1975), p. 109; and St. Catherine of Siena, *The Dialogue: The Classics of Western Spirituality* (New York: Paulist Press, 1980).

24. St. Teresa of Avila, "The Way of Perfection," in *The Collected Works of St. Teresa of Avila*, especially ch. 21, pp. 117–21.

25. St. Catherine of Genoa, *Purgation and Purgatory: The Classics of Western Spirituality* (New York: Paulist Press, 1979). See fn. 1 in ch. 1 of this book for a specific reference to the "instinct for beatitude."

4

Blessed Are Those Who Hunger and Thirst for Righteousness, for They Shall Be Satisfied

O God, you are my God whom I seek
for you my flesh pines and my soul
thirsts like the earth, parched,
lifeless and without water.
Thus have I gazed toward you in the
sanctuary to see your power and your
glory
For your kindness is a greater good than
life; my lips shall glorify you.
Ps. 63:2–4

Introduction

The proclamation in the first part of this Beatitude says rightly that we are people who hunger and thirst, yet the promise in the second part implies that satisfaction is not attained by finite means alone. To be human is to be spirit; it is to be more than a mere body. Hence our hunger and thirst, to be satisfied, demands more than physical food, even more than the satisfaction of performing a task well. The gratification of vital needs and functional ambitions still leaves us thirsty. The deepest thirst to be fulfilled orients us toward a transcendent horizon.[1] Only if we can find the righteousness, integrity, wholeness, and holiness this Beatitude promises shall we have our fill.

As spirit, human beings long ultimately for the fullness of peace and joy.[2] While we may glimpse this fullness at times, we shall not experience it totally in this life. All we may be granted now is a foretaste of what we shall enjoy fully then. Since neither the pleasure of gratifying sense appetites nor the satisfaction of functional ambitions can grant us the fullness of peace and joy promised in this Beatitude, to live it formatively will lead us into another purgative experience.

Desiring Goodness and Truth: The Human Foundation

To understand the purgative nature of this Beatitude, we need to uncover its human foundations. Perhaps a clue to this search can be found in the language of the text. The terms in our translation are *hunger* and *thirst*.[3] The object of this hunger and thirst is holiness, righteousness, or integrity, the desire for which shall be fulfilled. As is typical of spiritual language, these terms are both metaphorical and relational.

As metaphor, the words of blessing point to an experience that cannot be adequately expressed.[4] We can only say what it is *like* to search for holiness: it is like being hungry and thirsty at one moment and having that hunger and thirst satisfied at another.

Just as our bodies need food to survive, so does our spirit need to know and pursue the good, that is, to follow what is consonant with our foundational human formation. As our stomachs feel empty when we are hungry, so we feel unhappy when we witness lack of justice, peace, and mercy. It depletes our dignity to live uncongenial, incompatible, and compassionless lives.[5] Our transcendent hunger is as real as its vital counterpart. There is in us an innate desire to see and do what is right. It is this desire that leads us to give each person his or her due, to respect human rights and dignity, to resist whatever lowers our chances to live a good life.

Just as our bodies need water to preserve life, so we thirst in mind and heart to appraise and appreciate what is true, that is, to follow a way of life in tune with the whole of reality and not merely one perspective. We want to drink at the wellspring of Truth itself. As a person dying of thirst can think of nothing but a drink, so we experience a basic need to find and follow the most formative way of perceiving, thinking, appraising, and living. Experience teaches us that we cannot make snap judgments. If what we perceive is deceptive and deformative, then dissonant decisions and actions follow. Hence we thirst to be reflective, to make the best choices, to distrust what is impulsive and dystonic.[6]

As human beings gifted with the formation powers of transcendent mind and will, we are free to appraise situations and make choices.[7] Transcendent mind and will seek what is true and good. These powers of the spirit are activated by a desire to fulfill formative ideals continually appraised in light of one's life situation and attained only partially in this life.[8] Though we can create inner and outer conditions conducive to fulfillment, we cannot bring our own desires to closure. Hence we speak of the quest for congeniality, compatibility, and compassion, of the search for consonance with all that is, of the longing for wholeness and holiness. Just as we must eat and drink day by day to live, so we must go on seeking goodness and truth until we die.

On our formation journey we are drawn toward whatever promises satisfaction (power, pleasure, possession), and yet, once attained, these leave us unfulfilled. Just as we eat and then feel hungry a few hours later, so on the spiritual plane we may feel momentarily content, but soon we feel our basic incompleteness again. This feeling thrusts us toward a relationship with that which is beyond us.

Even physically we must go outside ourselves to find food and drink. We are not self-sufficient in that regard. Similarly, the wholeness we desire is not something we can give ourselves. It happens in relation to another. Though we may love and like ourselves, we still depend upon the affirmation others give us. Then, too, the integrity we seek for ourselves is sought for our fellow human beings as well. We bear interformative responsibility for one another.[9] When something disturbs a relationship, we want to smooth things over. Thus our search for wholeness is not a selfish endeavor; it involves the human community; it is relational. When others suffer, so do we. When others enjoy their fill, we are satisfied too, for looked at globally, we all share the same gift of life and all of us, as human beings, feel the call of consonant formation.

In the deepest sense, this Beatitude expresses the relation that exists between the human spirit and the Transcendent. Our physical hunger is often portrayed as symbolic of our hunger for intimacy with the Divine, our physical thirst as symbolic of our desire for eternal happiness. Union with the Divine Other makes possible our communion with one another and with creation. Thus fulfillment is possible only when we turn to the Eternal Source.

According to van Kaam, the aspiration to pursue the blessed life carries us beyond historical-cultural pulsations, beyond vital impulses and functional ambitions.[10] Since it cannot be fulfilled by any human source, the hunger and thirst for holiness is a purgative experience. Every occasion of satisfaction gives way to a new level of need. When our desire to drink from the wellspring of life is not satisfied, it feels as if we are dying. Hence our quest continues. In our desperation, we cry out to the Holy, knowing that the Divine Other alone can relieve us. Our condition awaits a healing touch. We cannot be our own redeemers. In this humbling awareness, in this purgation, we are thrust beyond ourselves toward the Transcendent.

Longing for the Holy: The Religious Articulation

> *As the hind longs for the running waters,*
>   *so my soul longs for you, O God.*
> *Athirst is my soul for God, the living God.*
>   *When shall I go and behold the face of God?*
> *My tears are my food day and night,*
>   *as they say to me day after day,*
> *"Where is your God?"*
>
> *Why are you so downcast, O my soul?*
>   *Why do you sigh within me?*
> *Hope in God! For I shall again be thanking him*
>   *in the presence of my savior and my God.*
>   *(Ps. 42:1–6).*

This psalm depicts the love relation between the soul and the Sacred that animates the religious person's entire life. Though the

One we seek at times hides himself, he is still our hope for fulfillment.

What attracts us to God? What keeps drawing us back despite
his apparent absence? In Judaism, the answer is his faithfulness.
He established a covenant of love with Israel, and he will not
abandon his chosen people, no matter how many times they disobey him. His message is clear, his fidelity unwavering. If we
respond in obedience, we can count on his nearness. We can trust
that he will relieve our hunger for holiness.

Any call issued to God from the abyss of human dependency
will be heard. Seekers who are not seduced to rest in anything less
than God will find him. That is the promise of faith. While we
are thinking of ways to reach and please him, he is already touch-
ing and fulfilling us. Not only does he reach out to love us; he
seems to draw us to holiness despite our resistance.

Our response to this love play is best expressed in an attitude
of humble submission. We allow him to have his way with us
rather than clinging to human anticipation. In short, one is pos-
sessed by God, not possessive of him. By surrendering to this
purgative hunger and thirst, we free ourselves from deformative
attachments and can more readily follow these innate transcendent
promptings to appraise and do what is spiritually right.[11]

Rather than follow their own will, religious persons in their
hunger and thirst for God keep his will ever before their eyes.
The Divine Will guides their living. Obedience to his call becomes
the goal of their quest. Self-love and formation ignorance diminish as one becomes more aware of the true nature of transcendent
formation.[12] Motives of selfish gain are set aside and we begin to
consider what must be done according to the dictates of justice
and integrity.

Say I am offered a higher position in my company on the condition that I promote the unjust labor practices of the foreman
who has just retired. While I want the added prestige the position
will bring, I know I should not compromise my principles regarding fair wages for all competent employees regardless of their race.
What should I do? If I listen to the spirit of justice, then the choice
is really no choice. I have to do what is holy and right in God's
eyes. I cannot profess belief in him and then act in opposition to

his will. If I remain faithful, I might have some influence on future company policy, but if I compromise, dishonesty and injustice will prevail.

Religiously motivated persons try to root out whatever deformative dispositions prompted them to act unjustly in the first place. As persons who thirst for what is right, they want to follow not only the prescriptions of the law but also its spirit. Only then will their outer actions reflect inner integrity. For religious persons, holiness cannot remain an exclusive relationship between us and the Transcendent. It must extend to other persons as well, for the Beatitude blesses all who hunger and thirst for holiness. The promise is as clear as the warning:

> *He who walks in the way of integrity*
> *shall be in my service.*
> *He shall not dwell within my house*
> *who practices deceit.(Ps. 101: 6–7)*

This movement away from deceit, egoism, and selfish inclinations constitutes a major struggle in the Christian experience. It is in the end impossible to appraise and follow the path of holiness without the spirit of Christ. Only his presence can satisfy our inmost desires. "Seek first his kingship over you, his way of holiness, and all these things will be given you besides" (Mt. 6:33).

Fulfilled in the Lord: The Christian Articulation

The Lord drew upon basic human experiences to help his followers understand the quest for holiness. When the people were hungry, he fed them, thus showing them that the satisfaction of hunger facilitates growth in faith. He respected people who functioned well in society like soldiers and fishermen, thus showing that work done well is good for the soul, especially when we place our talents at the service of higher ideals like service to the kingdom of God. The Lord blessed with special affection those who displayed great faith in the face of hopeless human situations. In them he beheld an insatiable quest for holiness that he held up as a model for others to emulate. These are the ones whose faith can move mountains, the people who will not forget the promise of ages. They did not walk away when he told them that he was the bread of life, that anyone who comes to him will never be hungry, that anyone who believes in him will never thirst (Jn. 6:34–40).

Jesus' sacrifice is what justifies us before the Father. As St. Paul teaches, we are justified not through our own works, nor through obedience to the law, but through the free gift of his Cross (Rm. 3:21–31). Christ sacrificed his life so that through him we would be reconciled with the Father. Faith in him is what makes us holy. Without his presence in us, we would have nothing to boast about. Moreover, faith gives the law its true value. A common distinction between a lower and a higher kind of righteousness may clarify this point and shed further light on the Beatitude we are considering.

Righteousness in Jesus' time had come to be associated mainly with the legalistic standards set by the scribes and pharisees. The wise love of the law, characteristic of former generations, had degenerated into paying lip service to rules and written codes. For instance, holiness was measured by the amount of money one donated to the temple. The awe-inspiring relation of Yahweh, highlighted in the Hebrew Scriptures, had been reduced to dispassionate quibbling over finer and finer points of the law. The pharisees were more concerned with the impression they were making on their peers than on caring for the needy and the maimed. In parables like that of the Good Samaritan, the Lord condemned this degeneration of God's law (Lk. 10:25–37). Lost was its spirit of love; only the shell of external meaning remained. This legalism promoted a lower idea of righteousness and made the quest for holiness at best lukewarm.

The Lord did not intend in any way to abolish the law (Mt. 5:17–18). His mission was to condemn the way it was interpreted and lived by hypocrites who showed off their external obedience but were empty of inner goodness. Jesus calls the scribes and pharisees blind leaders (Mt. 15:14). He resists their every attempt to trap him because he knows their wisdom is only surface deep. They have nullified God's words. They do not hunger and thirst for holiness, as do the poor in spirit. They think they have their fill, but the Master tells them how putrid and empty they really are (Mt. 23:1–8). Jesus reminds them of a shocking truth, that the greatest among them is the one who serves the rest, that whoever exalts himself shall be humbled, but whoever humbles himself shall be exalted (Mt. 23:12).

The kind of righteousness that clings to the letter of the law but ignores the loving intention within it will not save us. Hence, in this Beatitude, Jesus proclaims a higher ideal of holiness, one that affirms that God attends first to the state of a person's heart. If that is sound, then the words and actions that flow forth will reflect the goodness of God himself. This kind of righteousness challenges many of our assumptions and forces us to reexamine our intentions. For instance, Jesus says, "You have heard the commandment, 'You shall not commit adultery.' What I say to you is: anyone who looks lustfully at a woman has already committed adultery with her in his thoughts . . ." (Mt. 5:27–28). Thus, as van Kaam says, intraformation becomes the key to just and honest inter- and outerformation. If the heart is transformed, actions reflecting inner holiness will follow. If someone's heart remains hardened and convinced of its own self-imposed righteousness, he already has his reward. Because such a person is so full of himself, there is no room left in him for God to fill.

Characteristic of the higher righteousness Jesus proclaims is that it liberates the Christ form. It frees us from the vexing claims of revenge to offer the other cheek; from the spiteful clutches of greed to bind our brother's wounds; from the doubts of the rational mind to believe, even when we do not see. In short, we are freed to be who we fully are: God's servants, friends, children. Now, instead of focusing on our guilt before God, we can focus on divine generosity, on the mercy and forgiveness of God, on his promise to make us holy.

Though in this life we have to struggle to overcome sin, our efforts are sustained by his grace. Baptism gives us a new life in Jesus, and thus we can consider ourselves dead to sin and live for God (Rm. 4:1–25). Here again we see the connection between purgation and promise. The tension between human limit (sin) and divine possibility (grace) came to rest on the Cross.

The cross does not show what men did to God but what God does for us in this warfare between the forces of death and the call to new life. The Cross changes our understanding of redemption. It is not our doing that saves us, but the mercy and forgiveness of God. Only through this purgation of the Cross can we in turn follow the path to glory.

If the Cross was the crowning act of human injustice, it was paradoxically the most adequate expression of the justice of God. Jesus' own hunger and thirst were not satisfied until he had fulfilled the Father's will to completion. Our longings for holiness can only be filled when we follow the same way of surrender. The answer to injustice is best found in peaceful witness to what is right, despite the cost. It is this kind of witness that will help to redeem the world and reawaken the universal hunger and thirst for holiness.

Practical Applications of This Beatitude in Ongoing Formation

Our formation in this Beatitude finds fruition in a kind of second birth in which, to quote Adrian van Kaam, we put aside our pride form, lost in sin and prone to follow illusory desires, and put on a new self, the Christ form, created in the goodness and holiness of truth.

Obstacles

It follows from this that we must try to avoid any forms of lower righteousness, as if a tallying up of all we have done and are doing for God will make us holy. This mentality leads us to plan and propose transformation projects that fail in the end because they are generated by a self that refuses to accept its own vulnerability.[13] Without grace, all our efforts are in vain.

To surround ourselves by achievements or possessions, relying on these for security and proof of holiness, is to have had our fill already. Our lack of faith and trust is evident whenever we look to things outside of God to make us feel spiritually secure instead of to God himself as our only ultimate fulfillment.

Conditions

The Lord gives us a new set of directives by which to form our lives. For instance, we are never to let the sun go down on our anger. We are to guard against hostile and salacious words. We are not to bear grudges against others or lose our temper and be spiteful. On the positive side, we are to be kind and forgive others as readily as God forgives us. Not only must we believe in the Lord; we must be ready to suffer with him (Eph. 4:25–32). St. Paul sums up these directives when he writes: "God has not called us to immorality but to holiness; hence, whoever rejects these instructions rejects, not man, but God who sends his Holy Spirit upon you" (1 Th. 4:7–8).

Obviously, the way of higher righteousness begins with the awareness that we are sinners in need of his salvation. As our hearts abide with God, so our interior holiness grows. The fire of his love purges us of pride and inspires us to choose what he would do in our relations with others. Contrary to egocentric claims of self-reliance, we dwell frequently on our dependence on God, seeking with his grace to live purer, holier, more effective lives, despite daily hardships.[14] This intimate fellowship with the Lord reminds us daily that he is the source of all blessedness. Should we forget that he alone is capable of meeting the infinite desire of man with lasting satisfaction, we remember his saying:

> *I myself am the bread of life.*
> *No one who comes to me shall ever be hungry,*
> *no one who believes in me shall ever thirst.*
>
> (*Jn. 6:35*)

Notes

1. Adrian van Kaam, "Transcendent Detachment," *Studies in Formative Spirituality* 3 (1982): 140.

2. Adrian van Kaam, "Fullness of Peace and Joy," *G, Studies* 1 (1980): 296.

3. William Barclay speaks of "The Bliss of the Starving Soul" in his presentation of *The Beatitudes and the Lord's Prayer for Everyman* (New York: Harper & Row, 1963), p. 48.

4. Paul Ricoeur, *The Rule of Metaphor: Multidisciplinary Studies of the Creation of Meaning in Language,* trans. Robert Czerny (Toronto: University of Toronto Press, 1979).

5. See Adrian van Kaam, "Congeniality Manifestation," *G, Studies* 3 (1982): 143; "Apt Appraisal and Expression of Incompatibility Tensions," *G, Studies* 3 (1982): 144; Expression of Gentle and Compassionate Concern and Affection," *G, Studies* 3 (1982): 144; and "Result of this Dissonance," *G, Studies* 3 (1982): 126.

6. See Adrian van Kaam, "Deformative Effects of Human Form Directives," *G, Studies* 3 (1982): 302.

7. See Adrian van Kaam, "Explanatory Charts of the Science of Foundational Formation," *G, Studies* 2 (1981): 133–34, especially, Charts II and III.

8. I am indebted here to Adrian van Kaam for his distinction between formation ideals and formation projects.

9. "Interformative situations tend to evoke awareness of one's responsibilities for the transcendent formation of others." See Adrian van Kaam, "Evasion of Interformative Responsibility," *G, Studies* 1 (1980): 460.

10. See Adrian van Kaam, "Explanatory Charts of the Science of Foundational Formation," *G, Studies* 2 (1981): 136–38, especially, charts V/A–C.

11. See Adrian van Kaam, "Formative Attachment" and "Deformative Attachment," *G, Studies* 1(1980):150–51. *Formative attachment* is a commitment to formative directives that are relevant and effective in the present period or situation of life, while *deformative attachment* is a clinging to worn-out formation directives no longer relevant and effective in a period or situation of life.

12. Adrian van Kaam, "Formation Ignorance," *G, Studies* 1 (1980): 458.

13. "We should be disposed to appraise all exalted projects not only for what they are but also as potential points of entrance for demonic mini-obsessions." Adrian van Kaam, "Quasi-Transformation Projects," *G, Studies* 2 (1981): 535.

14. See Malcolm Muggeridge, *Something Beautiful for God* (London: Collins, Fontana Books, 1971). Mother Teresa is an outstanding witness to the human capacity to foster Christian formation under the most trying circumstances.

5

Blessed Are Those Who Are Persecuted for Righteousness' Sake, for Theirs Is the Kingdom of Heaven

The Lord God has given me
a well-trained tongue,
That I might know how to speak to the weary
a word that will rouse them.
Morning after morning
he opens my ear that I may hear;
And I have not rebelled,
have not turned back.
I gave my back to those who beat me,
my cheeks to those who plucked my beard;
My face I did not shield
from buffets and spitting.

Is. 50:4–6

Introduction

It is a rainy, cloud-covered day in Tasmania, the southernmost state of Australia. Everything looks bleak. The air is chilly, and I feel upon approaching this place that my melancholy mood matches the day perfectly. This is Port Arthur, ruins of a military compound and penal colony where over thirty thousand convicts were incarcerated from 1830 to 1883. Their crimes were as major as murder, as minor as stealing a loaf of bread to feed a starving family. Many were arrested in the British Isles, enchained and herded aboard ships, bound for what must have then seemed like the end of the world. It was surely the end of life as they had known it. After months of sailing under inhuman conditions, the survivors disembarked on the desolate south coast of the Tasman Peninsula, only to be caged again in cells that were hardly big enough to contain a man.

The ruins seemed to echo with their cries. Was it the howling wind I heard or the ancient wail of the persecuted whose dust saturated this grass? As I walked in the cold mist from rampart to rampart, I wondered how these prisoners or any like them could have found meaning in life. I passed a spot called the "Isle of the Dead" with unmarked convict graves. As these men watched one another waste away, could they believe there was anyone who loved them? Could such stark and inhuman persecution be spoken of in the same breath with blessedness?

My eyes until that moment had been focused on the ground. I was lost in my thoughts. Suddenly I rounded a corner of the compound and stood still. There, rising in the middle of this fortress, was the framework of a Gothic chapel, its spires stretching upward in transcendent beauty. Though it was raining harder now, I felt as if the sun had broken through. I ran to my guide and asked him for the history of the church. He told me the design had been executed by one of the prisoners, who must have been a gifted architect. His drawings were done on scraps of paper and a crew of fellow prisoners helped with the building.

The tourists I was with moved to another section of the encampment, but I stayed there. I stood still and listened. Could it be that the moans I heard before were really prayerful sighs sent heavenward by these aspiring souls? True, their bodies could be chained, but not their spirits. They were starved and beaten, but some deeper dignity in them lived on. Their church was a tribute to the human spirit, to its indomitable ability to seek meaning, however profound its suffering.

Seeing that chapel changed my day. It became a symbol of transcendence. In the midst of affliction, the soul had taken flight. The vision of that imprisoned architect would live on forever in these noble spires. With such tributes to transcendence, we have no need to fear. One is always free to find meaning amidst misery. When this meaning is centered in the mercy of God, shores as ancient as those of the Tasman Sea sing with a message of hope and glory—the message of this Purgative Beatitude.

It begins with a proclamation that is in itself paradoxical, for it blesses those who are persecuted on the condition that they suffer for the sake of holiness. This is like saying that purgation is for the sake of illumination. If one can find a meaning in suffering, then it is possible, despite terrible odds, to hope. We can believe the promise that the reign of God belongs to such people—a promise symbolized for me in the convict-built church of Port Arthur.

This Beatitude initiates a search for the meaning of suffering and persecution. It holds out the possibility that through these events, we can attain a kind of bliss that defies logical explanation.[1]

Does Persecution Cast Us Down or Raise Us Up?
The Human Foundation

As sure as we live, we shall have to undergo certain trials during the course from birth to death. Some are inevitable: family troubles, illness, the aging process. Others are unexpected: a car accident, a heart attack. Whatever the case may be, we find ourselves in a situation that has been cast upon us. What attitude do we take? Do we allow this pain or problem or persecution to overwhelm us? Must the feeling of being cast down become a prevailing mood or is there another alternative?

Our first response to suffering may be anger. We want to lash out at the source of our trouble. When acceptance does set in, we may start to worry excessively. What does the future hold? As the reality of this condition hits us, it may render us numb for a while. Only later, with reflection, is it possible to find opportunities for growth in these circumstances. We may look upon them as challenges to see our limits in a new light and learn to live within them. We let go of anger and needless worry and flow with reality. In due time, we may see that persecution does have a purpose. If we can endure it graciously, it may give us insight into the transcendent nature of human freedom.

People who allow suffering to raise them up to new heights of nobility usually grow more open, wise, and gentle than those who fight it or flee from it. Their self-understanding enables them to understand and console others. Because they believe that what is happening to them has a definite purpose, they can appraise more fully the part suffering plays in the overall pattern of human life. They can assure us that with time and reflection the purpose of persecution will become clear.

To gain access to the possible meaning of these purgative experiences, it is helpful to reflect upon some sources of persecution and suffering in the human condition. Can we enter into them for the sake of going beyond them? In other words, can we find transcendent meaning in apparent meaninglessness?

The Persecution of Our Basic Incompleteness. The human being is a broken unity. We are like amphibious creatures, with one foot on the land of the finite and the other in the sea of the infinite. No matter how hard we try, we cannot seem to find any means of autonomous fulfillment. To find ourselves, we have to go outside ourselves. We need others to affirm us. We need a higher purpose for which to live or for which to sacrifice our lives. If there is no love, no meaning out there, why live? If there is only frustration, disappointment, and despair, why not commit suicide?

There seems no other way to cope with such contingency than to take some kind of an inner stand toward it, while at the same time placing our trust in at least one other person. Somewhere we must find someone who loves us if we are going to be able to love our own limits and, consequently, to realize the possibilities of freedom allotted to us. Let me make this point clear by recalling a true story.

Once, when I was giving a talk, I spotted in the audience the face of a woman who appeared quite attractive. She looked soft and gentle and had an eager, receptive look in her eyes. It was almost as if I were speaking only to her. Often our eyes would meet, in confirmation of this affinity. Thus I was pleased when she came up after the lecture and asked if we could talk together. We walked to an adjacent parlor and sat face to face. Before a word was exchanged between us, she became misty-eyed. I wondered if I had offended her in any way. "Oh, no," she assured me. "It was as if you were speaking directly to me." What, then, had she wanted to see me about? What she said next startled me, because it was a rather intimate question. I suspect she could only ask it because we were strangers and the chances of our seeing each other again were remote.

Shyly she asked, "Do you like my face?" I was momentarily taken aback, but answered honestly. "It's strange that you should ask that because even while I was speaking I noticed your face. I thought of you as a gentle, lovely person and also felt at times as if I were talking to you." I paused and then asked, "Why did you want to know?" She lowered her eyes and said, "But didn't you notice how pockmarked and ugly my complexion is? I think I have a repulsive face."

I was a bit shocked by her poor self-image and could spontaneously assure her that her complexion had nothing to do with my liking her face. Now that she called attention to it, I did notice its imperfection, but so what? That did not detract from the quiet, gentle person she was. Had she ever thought that perhaps her suffering because of this bad skin was what made her so soft and receptive? Could there not be some good in what she had identified solely as a limit?

We talked for a while and at last came to grips with the deeper problem of impoverished self-esteem. In parting, I asked her to do me a favor the next morning when she arose and went to the bathroom to wash her face. I asked her to take a good look in the mirror, find her reddest pimple, put her finger on it and say, "I love you, little pimple." For in being able to love her pimple, she would be able to love her limits, and in loving her limits, she would come to love herself in her basic incompleteness. For our limits are the gifts that make us unique. By accepting our suffering from all kinds of lacks and rising above them, we cease to live in the illusion of disembodied angelism (everything should be perfect!) or sheer fatalism (nothing is ever right!).

The Persecution of Our Unfulfilled Expectations. We live life as time-bound creatures, tending toward what is to come while bending back on what was. We have the power to be in the present, to remember the past, and to project into the future. Thus we form certain expectations about what should be. We base these expectations on what life is now and on what it was then—making careful calculations and wagers on what shall be. The only problem is that we are not in control of the outcome. Despite our projections, the future may collide with the past and the present and produce the unexpected. Surprises that in no way conform to our expectations await us at every turn. Fond hopes are dashed against the harshness of reality. Health, wealth, fame, beauty . . . all go up in smoke. What happens then? Do we give up or revise our interpretations? We are free to go either way—that's what is so awesome about suffering. It determines us, but we also can and must taken an attitude toward it.

If we stop to consider daily life, we see how we are constantly persecuted by our unfilfilled expectations. We plan to write two chapters, but the telephone rings every five minutes and we get only two pages done. We wait for our friend to show up at lunchtime, only to find that he thought our appointment was yesterday. Perhaps the answer is to stop *waiting for* things and to start *waiting upon* reality as it unfolds moment by moment. This seems to be a more creative alternative than clinging fearfully to past determinisms or expecting wistfully the fulfillment of future dreams. The suffering associated with waiting is a good teacher, provided we are open to its message.[2] One of the blessings of living through such purgation is that we become more attentive to reality. We live less out of anticipation and more in tune with the everyday. But then, this leads to the next problem.

The Persecution of Everydayness. A kind of suffering is associated with the sheer living of ordinary routine. Getting up in the morning, going to work, coming home at night . . . growing old. Where does the time go? Is there any meaning to this dull pace of duty? When routine gets to us, we can choose to be bored or—to play on this word—to bore deeper into the meaning of passing time. Most of the time, life is not spectacular. It runs its course with a fair amount of regularity. And yet, if we pay attention to it, ordinary life can light up with new meaning.[3] There are wonderful things to be seen in the structure of a lettuce leaf if we hold it up to the light and take a good look.

Though living as ordinary people is a purgation, especially in an era like our own that promotes the fantastic and raises expectations of fulfillment, this same living can be an opening to reality in its true simplicity and flawed but awesome beauty.[4] Would the Grand Canyon be what it is if all the crags were cut straight?

When we behold the everyday, sensitive to its richness, we feel inwardly renewed.[5] We become freer to care in a gentle way for all persons and things.[6] We try to make each day count for something, whether anyone notices our efforts or not. Behind the apparent dullness of daily life, we discern a deeper meaning. Somehow each passing moment becomes an expression of the eternal. In this way, the purgation inherent in day-to-day existence bestows upon us a profound purpose.

Here again, we stand at the crossroad between mere limits or limits as possibilities. Any form of affliction can cast us down or raise us up. It all depends on our attitude. Persecution is a challenge to our freedom. We can choose to wallow in misery or, through pain, to become wiser. It is more certain that purgation will be an opening to illumination if we see life itself as a pointer to the transcendent—in short, if ours is a faith perspective. Then we can hear not only the paradoxical proclamation of this Beatitude but also its promise—that the reign of God will be ours. In the words of the poet George Herbert, "Affliction shall advance the flight in me."[7] This truth was brought home powerfully to me during a visit to the concentration camp of Dachau. There I was challenged, as at Port Arthur, to find meaning in a situation that stank of meaninglessness. As I walked through the compound, I found it necessary to draw upon all of my inner resources. From this experience emerged the following poem. I hope it reveals the depth of faith and hope necessary to illumine the darkness of human iniquity.

I.
Low over Dachau
  drop clouds of dark mist.
Our spirits dampen
  despite a deeper faith.

A demonic presence
  pervades this place.

No other words can contain
   horrors cruel as . . .

Barracks built to encage animals
   who once were men,
Gas chambers disguised as showers
   to cleanse away their cumulated filth,
Crematoria fueled by emaciated hands
   and feet.

II.
There is no why
   to soothe our pain.
In pouring rain we walk
   stunned by wordless disbelief,
   shocked into near despair.
Is there no hope?
Dare we face darkness
   that excludes the light?
Dare we look the devil in the face?

III.
We walk until we find
   a holy place,
   rising like a phoenix in the ashes
   of a lonely tomb:
Carmel of the Holy Blood.
Here grace emerges out of gloom,
Here seeds wet with red
   grow green with hope again.

IV.
We pray in silence
   and we pray aloud.
   Father,
   God,
   Lover of all people,
   Deliver us from evil.

Show mercy to those oppressed.
Let this Dachau,
        dark doom of many,
        become a door to everlasting light.

V.
Gray mist drops
        lower over Dachau.
We pilgrims pass beyond the compound fence
        to freedom.
A soft sigh slips through our lips,
A wordless tribute to those interred within.
        Their death, though without why,
                is not in vain.
        Its meaning shall live on in us
                again. [8]

Persecution for the Sake of Holiness:
The Religious Articulation

Despite the persecution of incompleteness, of unfilfilled expectations, of the everyday, we as spiritual persons need to find a higher reason for living than mere useless suffering.[9] We believe that persecution can be an avenue to greater wholeness and holiness. If we can go through this time of darkness in hope and faith, it will be dispelled in some as yet unknown way. Thus to suffer for the sake of holiness readies us to meet the Holy.

Enduring persecution for a higher purpose may foster a religious awakening. An inexplicable joy may come out of the pain of being persecuted for doing what is right, even if others find our action offensive. To be faithful to what is just and good will never be popular. The crowd follows the easy way of will-lessness or willfulness, to quote van Kaam.[10] The believer chooses the more difficult path of living firmly by the will of the Lord.

Our innate dignity makes us sensitive to the insults of others, whether verbalized or spitefully implied. It hurts when people ridicule our religious life directives, but to endure such persecution patiently is a mark of this Beatitude. It calls us to go one step further. We are to reach the point where we can even rejoice when such things happen to us. We can be glad when we are insulted and misunderstood because we obey a higher authority, consonant with our foundational divine form of life. The sign that we are on the right track, one sign we can trust, is persecution. Usually the truth hurts. That is why people make fun of it, argue against it, and refuse to take its teachers seriously.

It helps in the face of persecution for holiness' sake to develop a sense of history. Others before us have suffered under far worse conditions for their beliefs. Look at the prophets and the martyrs. Others now are suffering slander, insults, even torture. This purgation may break the body, but history shows it strengthens the spirit. Why are we tried and tested? What does it mean from a religious point of view? Are these experiences always blessed? The answers depend upon the way in which we understand the Sacred or the Transcendent. Against this horizon, we can deal with the meaning of suffering in our personal history. In the West, three traditions have offered answers to these questions: the Greek, the Roman, and the Hebraic.[11]

In the literature and philosophy of the Greeks, one discerns a deep pessimism about human life. Greek tragedy portrays the fact that unhappiness is written into the heart of things. The fate of humanity is in the hands of the gods, by whom mortals are destined to be miserable. In the short span between birth and death, one must expect to live mainly in sorrow, and there is no use complaining about it. Do, and suffer nobly—that is the proper response to life. We must suffer to grow wise, and this wisdom consists mainly in the knowledge and acceptance of our tragic fate. When one faces without flinching the triple tragedy of birth, suffering, and death, one is purged of all illusion and a catharsis of sorts takes place. Experience, often of the bitterest kind, conveys a wisdom that enables a person to defy the gods, whose sole purpose is to test the person's strength so that he may become like a god himself.

The Romans, like the Greeks, admired the stoic capacity to scorn death and bear pain in the face of impossible odds. Their gods were as careless of people as were the gods of the Greeks. The obstacles one meets in life are put there by the gods to spur one's efforts, for the Romans held that humankind must reject the life of ease and accept the yoke of power. Either one conquered or was conquered. Hence persecution was a challenge to gain victory over the opposition. Through suffering, one achieved name and power. Immortality was directly proportionate to mortal achievement, to victory, whatever the cost. Monuments built in one's name were the only immortality one could hope for. The combination of noble birth and tough, selfless labor for the empire would grant one entrance to the realm of divinity. For such a gain, any amount of suffering could be endured.

The Hebraic teachings on suffering surpass these pagan views and prepare the way for the Christian revelation. These writings presuppose a covenant between God and his people. His promise to Israel holds firm, but the people disobey. For this reason, suffering is often depicted as a punishment for sin. For instance, we read in the Book of Exodus:

> . . . I, the Lord, your God, am a jealous God, inflicting punishment for their fathers' wickedness on the children of those who hate me, down to the third and fourth generation; but bestowing mercy down to the thousandth generation, on the children of those who love me and keep my commandments. (Ex. 20,5–6)

The contrast is clear: disobedience results in punishment, obedience in mercy. It also seems that the innocent are fated to suffer for the sins of their ancestors. Thus sin and suffering go hand in hand. Sometimes suffering is depicted as a discipline leading to maturity, as when Abraham's faith was tested by God's asking him to sacrifice Isaac. However, this solution to suffering, as either a punishment for sin or a school for maturing in faith, was not sufficient to explain the suffering of the innocent. Hence we come to the Book of Job, where the question of persecution is stretched to the breaking point. If God is good and merciful, as the Hebrew Scriptures pose, if he is ready to comfort repentant Israel (Hos. 6:1–2), how can one account for suffering inflicted upon those who have obeyed, whose faith is mature, who from all human points of view live an innocent life?

Job's reasonable friends can offer no real answers to these questions, because from the human vantage point there are none. Job's experience of suffering remains inexplicable by logical standards. He is only able to attain some peace when he asks for and is granted an exalted vision of God's mysterious, providential plan for the world. Without understanding, he sees that his suffering is part of some greater plan, that it is not to be questioned, that his response is to be one of humble repentance for even having tried to pierce these mysteries.

The mystery dimension of suffering thickens in another milestone text, the Servant Songs of Isaiah. Here we discover the depth of God's desire to restore us to his friendship. He so loves us that he will send a Servant to take up our sufferings and to redeem us from the deforming powers of sin and death. By offering himself as a holocaust, the rift between God and humans, caused by sin, shall be healed. In the Servant, humble resignation to the will of God, combined with a steady awareness of his mercy and love, will give to persecution a meaning it never had before. The Servant, by his self-sacrifice, will transform a situation of dissonance, estrangement, and transgression into one of consonance, friendship, and obedience. In this case, innocent suffering has a purpose in that it atones for sin. It has a transcendent meaning in that it restores our original nearness to God.

Thus this literature offers a new possibility for interpreting human suffering. One can see it as an experience of purification that instills in us a disposition of resignation to the will of God. At the time of pain or persecution, these happenings seem dreadful. Later, when we look back upon them with faithful eyes, we can see that such trials did not occur accidentally. This time of disciplining was for our own good. The Holy gave us this trial to help us grow: Are we not more aware of transcendent mystery? Are we not more sensitive to our place in relation to all that is and its mysterious Source?

This disposition of humility, combined with a steady awareness of God's presence and loving care, leads us through suffering to purification and illumination. Such is the royal road of religious deepening. If God chastens harshly, it is so that his glory may flood our whole being. He raises up those who are brought low for his sake. The basic good news of Israel's message to the world, as seen, for instance, in the story of Naomi and Ruth, is that affliction can be turned into joy—if our faith is deep enough. The history of Israel is replete with witnesses to this paradox of blessing in persecution that continues to the present time.[12] To suffer for the sake of holiness is to follow the path of fidelity and humble acceptance of the will of God, especially in the face of opposition and popular forms of idolatry.

Turning now to the Christian revelation, it seems that the higher a person stands in the order of being, the more likely it is that he or she will have to suffer deeply. It is as if a person is only perfected *as human* through suffering *as meaningful*. This link between persecution and selfless love reaches its culmination in the Word who became flesh. If even God had to suffer, it must mean that there is a cross at the heart of creation.

The Blessing of Affliction: The Christian Articulation

The Christian message established once and for all the bond between suffering and love, persecution and holiness. It affirms that fidelity to divine precepts is strengthened by such trials. Enduring life's hardships can teach us to be patient and to hope in what is not yet—in the promise of the coming reign of God. The paradox of this position is summarized by St. Paul:

> Through him [our Lord Jesus Christ] we have gained access by faith to the grace in which we now stand, and we boast of our hope for the glory of God. But not only that—we even boast of our afflictions! We know that affliction makes for endurance, and endurance for tested virtue, and tested virtue for hope. And this hope will not leave us disappointed, because the love of God has been poured out in our hearts through the Holy Spirit who has been given to us. (Rm. 5:2–5)

Christians can rejoice in spite of the things that grieve them, for such trials are sources of faith, hope, and love. These events are part of God's forming mystery for our lives. In fact, no true transformation of heart is possible without them.[13] If our faith is strong, we can cope with these experiences and grow through them, as Christ did. Moreover, nothing that we have to endure—no pain, insult, or injury—can be as devastating as that which he took upon himself for our sake.

Purification through persecution is thus an inescapable part of the Christian experience. It may take two forms: active and passive. Active purification means that we strive to reject any desire or attachment that separates us from the love of God. Passive purification means that the fire of God's love ultimately burns out of us the dispositions that lead to sin. The first kind of purification is preparatory, the second is transforming. The sight of our own wretchedness, coupled with an inner longing for God, accounts for the intermingling of suffering and love typical of the purgative way. Such trials enable us to follow God wherever he leads and to endure the persecutions incurred by obedience.

It is consoling to observe at all times the pattern of the Paschal Mystery. Just as Calvary led to the joy of Easter, so our trials last but for a season. They come and go as God sees fit. If we respond to them courageously, our formation in Christ will deepen. The cross is but a stopping place on the road to resurrection and the reign of God. We know from experience that God never tries us beyond our strength. Even if we falter once in a while and betray him, we go on believing in his forgiveness and forming plan for our lives. If at all times we cast ourselves confidently upon him, he will give us whatever grace we need to reach that final life form wherein the meaning of our entire faith journey will be made manifest.[14]

Purgation is not meant to diminish our dignity but to strengthen it immeasurably. It purifies us of deformative tendencies of the pride form that obscure the Christ-likeness to which we are called. Accepting our own crosses increases our capacity to live compassionately with others. This mystery of formative suffering prepares us for whatever mission God has in mind. In accepting the cross as the sign of our salvation, we become other Christs, a community of sufferers drawn out of our desolation toward the healing consolation of a compassionate God.

Now we can appreciate more fully the promise of this Beatitude that the reign of God shall be ours. Affliction for the Christian is not a curse but an occasion of transcendence. It is an opportunity to rise above our initial inclination to bear suffering stoically or to escape it altogether. Instead we identify with the crucified Christ and find new meaning in difficulties, persecutions, and defeats. To live suffering as a blessing allows us to enjoy the bliss of God's kingdom. We enter into our true homeland of likeness with Father, Son, and Holy Spirit. This reign may grant us little or no earthly power, for to be a conquering commander is not the way of Christ. Monuments to human fame are nothing in comparison with what it means to belong to the reign of God and to experience the grace of transforming union.[15] When Christ was brought to nothing, to the most profound depth of humility, his mission for the Father was consummated.

Likewise our formation journey must not consist in exalted spiritual feelings or the desire for some magical formula guaranteeing transformation. Rather it consists in embracing the cross. This self-emptying consumes the inordinate affections and sinful dispositions the soul has contracted throughout life. This purgation may last a long or a short time. It is up to God to decide. He allows this condition to persist until our spirit is humbled, softened, and purified enough to become a fit dwelling place for the Spirit of God. In the course of life, at various intervals, this kind of purgation may cease to assail the soul and God will shine forth as our innermost life and light. Such occasions of illumination signify the healthy condition purgation is effecting in the soul. These glimpses offer a brief but unforgettable sense of the fullness of peace and joy for which the soul longs.[16] In light of what we have beheld briefly, we learn more about the imprisoning power of the pride form and its resistance to God's transforming love. We see clearly our own poverty. According to the spiritual masters, God grants this depth of purgation to those whom he wishes to elevate to the highest degree of union.[17] St. John of the Cross insists that only the purest suffering can produce the purest understanding. In other words, the only way to attain union is the way of the cross.[18]

Practical Applications of This Beatitude
in Ongoing Formation

All of us are driven at times by impulses over which we seem to have no control. Our ambitions get the best of us. We forget our aspirations toward goodness, truth, and beauty. We reject or repress the inspirations of the Holy Spirit. We are caught in the pride systems that blind us to our innate vulnerability. Such familiar facts of life affirm the one main idea expressed in this Beatitude: Far from attempting to escape persecution, we ought to thank God for it. It is his way of training us to see that everything that happens to us has transcendent meaning.

Obstacles

As bodily creatures, we are programmed to protect ourselves. Our instinct is to avoid anything unpleasant. Unless we can overcome this tendency to flee the cross, we shall not enjoy the new life of grace God holds in readiness for us.[19] Part of the problem may be that we await the appearance of the cross in a dramatic form. We forget that the cross offers itself under the most ordinary disguises: a flat tire, a family disagreement, a birthday or anniversary forgotten. Whether these occasions are formative or deformative depends on how we live through these troubles. No one initially welcomes irritation and displeasure as potential sources of joy. Generally they seem contrary to human anticipations and appear mainly as obstacles.

In our blindness to spiritual meanings, we seek an instant solution to the suffering we feel. We don't pause to consider the deeper symbolism of what is happening. We hate to admit our vulnerability. We resent having to wait for something to be resolved in ways over which we have little or no control. We succumb to all kinds of distractions rather than sitting still to appraise this situation as a possible call to holiness. Whether seeking the easy way out or losing ourselves in busy work, we resist the ordinary trials of daily life. By the same token, as van Kaam insists, we miss the opportunities they grant us for purification of the pride form and the ignorance of transcendent formation it breeds.

Conditions

Growing in the spirit of this Beatitude means that we try neither to escape these forms of persecution nor to resist them. Rather we welcome them as avenues to Divine Presence, to the reign of God the Beatitude promises. The cross becomes for us a symbol of hope and freedom. The limitations revealed by suffering become indicators of our true strength. Instead of despising our infirmities, we accept them as messengers proclaiming that without

God we are and can do nothing. Once this recognition becomes part of our formation history, we can turn every occasion of persecution into an opportunity for transformation in Christ.[20]

Certain dispositions facilitate this transformation. We are able to resign ourselves to God's will in desolation as well as consolation. We live from a transcendent perspective in which we assign a formative meaning to every event of daily life. We believe with all our hearts that nothing falls outside the formation mystery. Suffering persecution, which may once have been a deformative source of vengeance and bitterness, now becomes an occasion for practicing resignation and trust.

Persecution for the sake of holiness becomes a bridge to the reign of faith, hope, and love—the "foundational triad" on which all Christian formation is built.[21] In faith, we believe that God watches over us with paternal/maternal care, giving us the courage to endure suffering as did his Divine Son. In hope, we accept these many moments of persecution as signs of our sharing in the redemptive compassion of Christ for mankind and world. In love, we embrace the divine forming plan for our lives. We adore the God who made us in his image and likeness, who holds us in being, and who draws us finally to the bliss of his kingdom.

Notes

1. See Viktor E. Frankl, *Man's Search for Meaning* (New York: Simon & Schuster, Pocket Books, 1963).

2. Simone Weil's characteristic attitude of informed waiting is philosophically expressed in *Waiting for God* (New York: Harper & Row, Colophon edition, 1973). For an interesting literary approach to "waiting for God" in the experimental theater mode, see Samuel Beckett's highly acclaimed *Waiting for Godot* (New York: Grove Press, 1954).

3. For a reflection on the way in which ordinary life lights up with meaning, see Annie Dillard, *Pilgrim at Tinker Creek* (New York: Macmillan Co., 1963); and Loren Eiseley, *The Unexpected Universe* (London: Penguin Books, 1973).

4. See Judith Guest, *Ordinary People* (New York: Ballantine Books, 1977).

5. See Susan Muto, *Renewed at Each Awakening: The Formative Power of Sacred Words* (Denville, N.J.: Dimension Books, 1979).

6. See Adrian van Kaam, *Spirituality and the Gentle Life* (Denville, N.J.: Dimension Books, 1974).

7. From "Easter Wings" by George Herbert, in *The Poems of George Herbert* (London: Oxford University Press, 1961).

8. Susan Muto, "Further Reflections on Formative Reading," *Envoy, Journal of Formative Reading* 18 (1981): 28–29.

Place
Stamp
Here

Epiphany Association
947 Tropical Avenue
Pittsburgh, Pennsylvania 15216-3031

Thank you for choosing this book.
If you would like to receive more detailed information about
the Epiphany Association, our resources and programs,
please fill in this card.

Please check the programs that are of particular interest to you:

☐ Associate Membership and Epiphany Associates' Retreat
(EAR)

☐ Epiphany Lay Formation Academy (ELFA)

☐ Epiphany Certification Program (ECP)

☐ Spiritual Formation for People in Ministry (IFM)

☐ *Epiphany International: The Journal of Formation Science
and Formation Theology*

☐ Complete Informational Packet

Name: _____

Address: _____

_____

9. See Jean-Paul Sartre, *Being and Nothingness* (New York: Washington Square Press, 1966). According to Sartre, "A dull and inescapable Nausea perpetually reveals my body to my consciousness."

10. See Adrian van Kaam, *Religion and Personality* (Denville, N.J.: Dimension Books, 1980), pp. 92–101.

11. See John Ferguson, *The Place of Suffering* (London: James Clarke & Co. 1972).

12. See Corrie ten Boom, *The Hiding Place* (London: Hodder and Stoughton, 1971). The strength of God's promise sustained Corrie and her sister through times of profound suffering and horror.

13. Adrian van Kaam, "Transformation of Heart," *Studies in Formative Spirituality* 1 (1980): 144.

14. Adrian van Kaam, "Characteristics of the Final Ideal Life Form of Christian Life," *G, Studies* 1 (1980): 295.

15. "Grace may lift a person in all formation dimensions into a pneumatic life of full consonance with the divine formation mystery. . . ." Adrian van Kaam, *G, Studies* 2 (1981): 510.

16. "In congenial formation the Divine Source of formation is progressively experienced and lived as the Fullness of Peace and Joy." Adrian van Kaam, "Fullness of Peace and Joy," *G, Studies* 1 (1980): 296.

17. "Before the divine fire is introduced into and united to the substance of soul through a person's perfect and complete purgation and purity, its flame, which is the Holy Spirit, wounds it by destroying and consuming the imperfections of its bad habits. And this is the work of the Holy Spirit, in which he disposes it for the divine union and transformation in God through love." See St. John of the Cross, "The Living Flame of Love" in *The Collected Works of St. John of the Cross*, trans. Kieran Kavanaugh O.C.D., and Otilio Rodriguez, O.C.D. (Washington, D.C.: Institute of Carmelite Studies, ICS Publications, 1973), p. 586.

18. Ibid, "The Ascent of Mount Carmel," pp. 123–24.

19. Peter Fransen, *The New Life of Grace* (New York: The Seabury Press, 1969), pp. 19–21.

20. See Dietrich von Hildebrand, *Transformation in Christ* (Chicago: Franciscan Herald Press, 1948).

21. For a reflection on the "foundational triad," see Adrian van Kaam, "The Open-Ended Christian Life Form," *G, Studies* 1 (1980): 295.

THE ILLUMINATIVE BEATITUDES

6

Blessed Are the Merciful,
for They Shall Obtain Mercy

*God who is mighty has done great things
for me,
holy is his name;
His mercy is from age to age
on those who fear him.*

Lk. 1:49–50

Introduction

The Purgative Beatitudes pertain mainly to the intraformative unfolding of the human person. They touch the heart in its quest for holiness. The experiences of mourning, hunger and thirst, and persecution present us with options to be appraised by transcendent mind and will. This appraisal passes through the provisional stage and results in concrete decisions and actions that move us, according to van Kaam, from one current life form to the next.[1] Experiences such as these directly confront the pride form. They purify us from illusions of mere self-sufficiency and enable us to know ourselves as we really are, that is, in the humility of the Christ form. All dimensions of our inner life, including memory, imagination, and anticipation, are affected by this purgation.[2] Because of the nature of these foundational human meanings, we are brought again and again to the threshold of choice between despair or hope, resentment or fidelity, cowardice or courage.

The Illuminative Beatitudes also articulate formative dispositions of the heart that are distinctly Christ-like. Who could be more merciful, gentle, and peace-loving than he? These dispositions not only facilitate intraformation in divine likeness. They also enlighten our interformative relations with others, and our outerformative relations with our immediate life situation and world.[3] Because they temper the exalted and exalting pride form, these attitudes enable us to identify more consistently with the Christ form in the core of our being and to become more worthy messengers of his word. As Christ taught us to love God with our whole heart and soul and our neighbor as ourselves, so these Beatitudes show us concretely how the mutual love between God and humanity extends itself in mercy, gentleness, and peace. By putting these attitudes into practice, we progress not only in graced self-formation but also in becoming better instruments of the Lord in the formation of others.[4]

The Illuminative Beatitudes indicate our deepening receptivity to pneumatic inspiration. They enable us, as St. Paul indicates in his Epistle to the Ephesians, to become children of the light. This inner lucidity illumines our situation and world as the light of a bonfire brightens the darkness around it. So, too, the Illuminative Beatitudes challenge us to grow more alight with the love of Christ and to kindle his radiance in others.

In this blessing there at first seems to be no paradox, for the text affirms that people who are good to others, who show mercy, are being their best selves, humanly speaking. If there is any problem, it resides in the promise, for though we may be kind to others, there is no guarantee that they shall show kindness to us in turn. Compassion requires taking a risk as well as believing that though one may not receive mercy in kind from others, one shall always receive mercy from God. We may be called fools for trying to become a healing presence in the world. People may perceive us as a threat to the inhumane notion of survival of the fittest. All we can do is keep on being kind despite the opposition, trusting that somehow, either now or later, the mercy God promises will be granted to us. We must believe that his kindness endures forever, that his mercy extends from age to age to those who love him.[5] In this experience of waiting upon the mercy of the Lord, the Illuminative Beatitude becomes mingled with a purgative component.

Responding with Mercy: The Human Foundation

We must admit that people can be horridly mean to one another. For some, unkindness is more the rule than the exception. We cringe at the mounting evidence of our capacity to dehumanize others, to rape, torture, kill. Something dies in us when we hear news reports about violence in the streets, teenage suicide, suppression, sudden captivity, execution without trial. Is there no end to the chaos and cruelty pervading our world? Or is all of this evidence that we need more than ever to restore compassion?

Compassion is rooted in the recognition of our common "alikeness," in the fact that we are like one another physically, functionally, and spiritually, though at the same time each of us is unique. We all have fingerprints, though each set of fingerprints is different. This essential "alikeness," or what we could call "kind-ness" (united by common traits), is the source of our capacity to see in the strengths and weaknesses of others something of ourselves.

However repressed the emotion of commonality or kindness may be, we still hope that even in the cruelest tyrant there resides some sense of respect for human dignity. We dread the moment when life is treated as a dispensable commodity. It seems as if the only corrective to this tragic loss of sensitivity to humankind is compassion. Human misery cries out for the response of mercy, for some healing moment. Even if this expression is material, as in giving food, clothing, or money to someone in need, it ought ideally to flow from that more transcendent sense of "suffering with" or compassion.

Compassion enables us to see behind external failings to the infinite value of the person. It celebrates the likeness we share as members of the human family. In compassionate exchanges, we experience what it is like to be with one another in a special way, to laugh together, to cry together, to rejoice and to weep. We sense deep down how alike we are. For no matter what status of life we have attained, our flesh burns when it touches flame. However brilliant or limited our minds may be, each of us attempts, at least in our best moments, to use our talents well. Whether we profess belief in a higher power or doubt such a possibility, our plea for some deeper meaning needs to be heard.

In these and other ways, compassion teaches us that we are part of one another, that we cannot be indifferent to our needs as a global family.[6] From the viewpoint of foundational human formation, two dimensions of being seem to stand at the base of this "family feeling." They are *kindness* and *communion*. The essential kindness that binds us together stems from the fact of our shared humanity. Upon further analysis, five dimensions of this foundational kind-ness disclose themselves.

The first is *empathy*. According to Webster, empathy is the imaginative projection of a subjective state into an object so that the object appears to be infused with it. The definition goes on to state that empathy is the capacity for participating in another's feelings or ideas. For instance, when I see a stranger in an airport whose worn-out face and slumped figure express my own feelings, I empathize with him. I project into his slouched and vulnerable posture what it feels like to be transported from meeting to meeting with no time for personal encounter. According to van Kaam, effective interformative presence to others requires empathy for their feelings and for the situations in which they find themselves. He sees a link between empathy, formative imagination, and interformation, stating that interformative imagination is a necessary means of putting oneself concretely into the inner and outer situation of any person with whom one hopes to interact formatively.[7]

Sympathy, the second expression of human kind-ness, means to have common emotions or experiences sparked by a susceptible or pathetic condition. Here the experience is not imaginative, as in empathy, but real and current. The instance of sympathy most readily recalled is our feeling for another who has lost someone dear through death and is now in mourning. Sympathy calls for some concrete way in which we can show our sorrow and offer support.

A third expression of kind-ness centers on the experience of *imitation*.[8] By imitation we mean a conscious attempt to model our life on the life of another whom we admire. We desire to imitate his or her attitudes toward living and to follow in some way the actions that such inner values and commitments generate. In other words, in the experience of imitation, like is drawn toward like. For instance, I like the way you treat other people. I admire your patience and ready ability to make the best of every situation rather than to grumble about the stupidity of others. I so admire your positive approach that I try to develop in myself the inner attitudes that promote such compassionate actions.

A fourth and deeper level of kind-ness is characterized by *intimacy*. For instance, in a warm, enduring friendship, there is a bond of affinity between our inner feelings, thoughts, and attitudes and those of another. We are kindred souls in a profound and lasting sense. In the case of "soul friends" or "soul keepers," we see a remarkable example of human intimacy.[9] Intimate friends experience a kind of gifted bonding between their emotions, ideas, and attitudes. Theirs is not an external, breakable bond but an internal bond of graced affinity. This means that while remaining fully unique beings who respect each other's transcendent selfhood, they feel themselves to be deeply at one. While not fusing with each other in a sickly, dependent relation, they feel maturely dependent on each other in ways that defy expression. So profound is their mutual reverence and respect, so myriad are the ways in which they help each other, that one friend feels incomplete without the other. Such intimacy between persons is often compared in spiritual traditions to the bond of selfless love between the soul and God.

An experience underlying all of the above, that of *identification*, expresses the fifth and final level of kind-ness. We identify or wish to identify with what is at the base of these various expressions of kind-ness or oneness. We trace them to the common source of our being as such. This sharing in being accounts for our ability to identify with one another in all of these ways. Thus identification is at the base of this "family feeling," fostering our capacity to be compassionate toward one another.

A second major dimension of membership in the human family concerns the mystery of communion or union between people—a communion rooted in shared vital, functional, and transcendent underpinnings. We can participate in one another's inner and outer life because all of of us share in a common structure. In the science of foundational human formation, this underlying structure or life form is seen as articulating itself in various dimensions that each and every one of us shares because of our common humanity.

These dimensions are: the *historical-cultural,* which locates us in a personal stream of history and a cultural setting; the *vital* or bodily form of biological animation and vital emotionality; the *functional,* which prompts us to manage our lives in a reasonable way and to pursue worthwhile ambitions, plans, and projects; the *transcendent,* which accounts for our aspirations for more profound meaning; and, in persons baptized by water or desire, the *pneumatic* dimension that receives into the human spirit the light and love of the Holy Spirit, who guides our appraisal of life's meaning in a God-oriented direction.[10]

On all of these life dimensions, we are in communion insofar as all of us participate in similar strivings. The science of formation designates these as: historical-cultural pulsations, vital impulses, functional ambitions, transcendent aspirations, and pneumatic inspirations.[11] To be in communion with others implies a common grounding in these dimensions and dynamics of human unfolding. A sense of communion leads to the kind of communication that respectfully takes into account the formation process going on within ourselves, and with our interformative communities, our immediate situation and world.

As formative appreciation and appraisal deepen, we necessarily grow more compassionate toward our own limits and the vulnerabilities of our fellow human beings. This foundational disposition implies the bonds of communion that underpin our interformation. Compassion signifies that we are in touch with the limits and potentialities of the human condition as such.[12] Because we are able to befriend our own vulnerability, we are able to respond mercifully to the limits of others.

In this light, we can identify three manifestations of the mystery of communion. The first is *fellow feeling*. Vitally, functionally, transcendentally, we sense our involvement with one another. In the words of the poet John Donne:

> No man is an island, entire of itself; every man is a piece of the continent, a part of the main. If a clod be washed away by the sea, Europe is the less, as well as if a promontory were, as well as if a manor of thy friend's or of thine own were: any man's death diminishes me, because I am involved in mankind, and therefore never send to know for whom the bell tolls, it tolls for thee.[13]

We may ignore or repress this fellow feeling at times, but in the end, it catches up with us, for no matter what our special talents or possessions, they cannot save us from the final bond that unites us with all other human beings: death. Fellow feeling grips us at this point and spreads out to include our shared joys and sorrows. It is expressed in the oft-heard phrase: "There but for the grace of God go I." These shared feelings may be the basis for the so-called corporal works of mercy, for it is an expression of good fellowship to feed the hungry and give drink to the thirsty, to clothe the naked and visit those sick and in prison.

The second manifestation of communion dives more deeply into the mystery of hidden union. As in the experience of intimacy, we are drawn into the hidden recesses of our being, where we all long for some kind of transcendent fulfillment. We know that no specific person, event, or thing can satisfy this longing. It goes beyond material solutions and aspires toward transcendence, toward the fullness of peace and joy. This desire may not be verbalized, but it always hovers beneath the surface of human formation as its lasting dynamic.

Perhaps it is this longing for union that stands behind the instance of communion originally stressed, that of *family feeling*. It is this feeling that accounts for the interformation without which human beings could not exist. We need one another from birth to death. This feeling draws us beyond ourselves toward others in our here-and-now associations and in the global community. It invites us, as van Kaam says, to participate as form-giving and form-receiving people in the quest for whatever facilitates human formation. This feeling of being with and for others beckons us beyond reflection to action, beyond solitude to encounter. It calls us to rise above initial narcissism and to open ourselves to the needs of others, generously and compassionately.

Because we are all members of one family, we accept the responsibility to respond to the vital, functional, and transcendent needs and feelings we sense in one another. This response is not diffuse but specific. It takes into account who we are and who the other is at this moment. It recognizes that the needs of some may be for material sustenance, while others may be spiritually deprived. We do not make prior judgments of what people need most but pay attention to the situation and to our own congenial and compatible gifts. Consonant formation and interformation require the blending of heart, mind, and will, of congeniality, compatibility, and compassion.[14] For instance, the service offered by a research scientist will be different from that given by a social worker. While the means of aiding others is unique, the motivation for so doing flows from this shared family feeling.

Compassionate persons thus respond to the call of others as wisely as they can, continually appraising each new situation. They are available to do something or simply to be with someone. They try to be present sensitively, unselfishly, tenderly, accepting the blessing and burden of our interformative responsibility. They may make their presence known or remain anonymous, whichever is best for others. Such persons are both giving and forgiving. Their care, concern, and respect transcend the boundaries of social status, race, place, culture, or belief. They go beyond these limits because of the limitless holy ground in which we all have our beginning. This ground of compassion is none other than the formation mystery that embraces all creation.

The Divine Ground of Mercy:
The Religious Articulation

The Source beyond us, binding us together, is the wellspring out of which mercy flows. In this Sacred Source, we feel ourselves linked with the whole of creation and with each particular expression of that creation. We blend with blades of grass as well as with fellow beings.[15] All seem dependent on a benevolent source from whom everything comes and to whom each is returning.

Human beings belong in principle, therefore, to the same divinely sustained family. Over a long course in the history of thought and formation, we have come to see this fact more clearly. For the modern consciousness, this commonality seems unquestionably clear since we have seen from outer space the fragile planet on which we all reside. Undoubtedly, this view of Earth has made it more possible for us to pledge ourselves to sharing.

For this reason, every concrete act of compassion, however slight, in whatever cultural setting, points beyond itself to a Source that is benevolent, to a limitless Forming Power that sustains the unfolding cosmos. Thus every gesture of mercy is blessed, if not by humans, then by a Loving Other, who cares for all created beings. To the degree that we have felt the healing touch of compassion through any corporal or spiritual expression of family feeling, we can posit behind this generous giving a Divine Giver. One act of mercy is enough to cancel the opposite view of a malevolent force that cares nothing for humanity, that sets the universe in motion and lets it run toward its own destruction. If we can move beyond egoistic claims and care for others, how much more must the Divine Other be a nurturing source of love, who ordains and sustains initial and ongoing creation?

This sense of the fatherhood and motherhood of God is confirmed in Christianity. God's own Word of kindness, his Son and our Savior, entered human history. His response to human maliciousness was to come into the world as the emissary of divine mercy. By accepting the Cross, a notorious symbol of inhumanity, he transcended a gross expression of human cruelty and transformed life into a mission of mercy.

Mercy Given, Mercy Shown: The Christian Articulation

With the appearance of Jesus, the merciful face of God, which was there from the beginning, was revealed in full. Jesus showed us once and for all that we are all members of one family. His actions insisted that mercy must be bestowed upon those in misery. He revealed the Father as a God of limitless love who cares continually for our well-being, as a God who is gracious and merciful, slow to anger and of great kindness, good to all and compassionate toward all his works (Ps. 145:8–9).

Basically, the Lord asks us to love one another as he has loved us—that means to be merciful, compassionate, forgiving. It means, if necessary, losing our life for the sake of those we love. The lesson of this Beatitude is perhaps best contained in the depiction of the Last Judgment, where Jesus assures his disciples that as often as they showed mercy to the least of his brothers and sisters, they did it for him, but that as often as they neglected the least of these, they neglected him (Mt. 25:40–45). The rule of Christian living is simple and unrelenting: "Be compassionate, as your Father is compassionate" (Lk. 6:36).

Whenever we show mercy to others, we express the Christ form of our being. This expression transforms the darkness of human misery in two main ways. First of all, we become more sensitive to the material and spiritual needs of our family members because now we see ourselves as members of Christ's Mystical Body. Second, we feel responsible to manifest our care concretely in Christian hospitality, by creating better standards of living for those in need, by helping all to grow in companionship with the Lord.

We must try to live in an attitude of mercy toward all and malice toward none. Following the example of Divine Compassion, we begin to feel that there is no sinner so evil as to be denied the offer of mercy and forgiveness. Even if the one who offends us does not appear to be repentant, we must still try to be forgiving. Without forgiveness, the weeds of resentment grow swiftly, choking off the tender shoots of mercy.

I am reminded here of a story of a great ruler who needed a second-in-command to help manage his kingdom. When he finally selected the right person, he took him outside onto a balcony of the palace from whence they could gaze over all the lands under his jurisdiction. His new helper asked the king, "Master, what must I remember most of all if I am to carry out your wishes?" "My son," the king replied, "there is only one directive to follow—and that is to look upon the people as wounded."

The Father saw our wounded condition since the Fall. He knew we could not cure ourselves. So great was his love that he sent his Son to heal our brokenness and to help us overcome obstacles to mercy. The mercy he extends to us must be extended to others. It is as if he invites us in this Beatitude to join hands and create a great chain of compassion that will encompass creation and drive out, wherever possible, evidences of human cruelty.

God sends us into the world to be compassionate with others in their broken condition, to minister to them as we would minister to Christ, to serve and not to be served. In compassion, we make no comparisons; we give up envious competition. We do not judge people according to their earthly achievement. Who knows who is holier in the sight of God? It is only our place to draw back into God those who are wounded, to reclaim those who are broken so that they may enjoy reunion with the Unbroken. Compassion aims to remove crushing burdens, to free one from fear, to foster the capacity to love. This is what Jesus did for us, and it is what we are to do for one another.

Practical Applications of This Beatitude
in Ongoing Formation

As Scripture and the spiritual masters teach us, the deepest failure we can incur in formation is our failure to love. This lack snuffs out the fires of compassion. It fans those of harsh judgment and inhumane behavior. The failure to love also shows up in little ways like impatience with children, angry flare-ups, the hesitancy to tell others we care. It is expressed in the labels we attach to others; in the defensive armor we wear to protect ourselves; in the "cat fights" that go on between us; in the gossip that replaces affirming remarks; in the domination of needy love over giving love; in the suppression of others for the sake of self-glory.

Obstacles

In further applying this Beatitude to practical formation, it may be helpful to review what mercy is *not*. It is not primarily a vital feeling. That is to say, it must be extended to others whether we feel a spontaneous liking for them or not. Compassion is more an expression of the will than of the emotions. In Christ, we must choose to love mercifully no matter how we may feel about a fellow member of the human family. Our love has to be shown in prudent actions that reflect the compassion of Christ, even if these acts of mercy require that we sacrifice our initial feelings of repulsion. A classic example of the kind of love that transcends initial aversion for the sake of Christ is found in the story of St. Francis of Assisi, who struggled to overcome his disgust and kiss a leper. Such love is not a matter of felt affinity but of steady care for others based on our beholding God in them.

It follows that the expression of compassion does not demand that we have a person-to-person relation with another. I may be compassionate toward people because of long-standing family or friendship ties, but I must try, with discretion, to show love to strangers. The disposition of compassion reaches beyond personal association toward all whom God places in our path. We must at least be open to the possibility of extending consolation toward all members of the human family, not merely a few select people.

Our formation in compassion does not rely on amiable togetherness. It is characterized by a kind of selfless caring for others that rests on a transcendent appreciation of their well-being. Expressions of mercy do not depend on surface needs. They penetrate externals to go to the core of our fallen condition. All people are vulnerable. To behold their need is to move from a love that is self-centered to one that is truly self-donating in whatever situation God places us. Such love is eternally fresh. It never places the other in a preconceived mold but respects his or her uniqueness. Thus we become truly sensitive to others' distress, trying to empathize with what they are going through, resisting the tendency to pass quick judgment, content to be with them in a supportive way on their formation journey.

Conditions

Compassion needs to be incarnated in concrete ways that manifest prudent responses to a given situation. For instance, though we forgive an "enemy" in our heart, we may have to wait for an opportune time to express this sentiment verbally. We may show respect for human dignity by feeding one person in a soup kitchen and another with the words of a fine sermon.

Compassion presupposes detachment from selfish traits combined with a growing attachment to the Lord. The inner channels of our ears and hearts must be cleared of such obstacles if we are to respond to the real needs of others. Some may be secretly wishing for a word of admonishment; they need firm formation direction. Others may have been too harsh on themselves; they need gentle support and a few words of praise.[16] In one case, a monetary donation is necessary; in another, only a quiet smile of reassurance. As our hearts are transformed in Christ, we will be better able to appraise what he wants us to say and do and be in each situation.

It is as important to learn to receive graciously the acts of kindness others show us. It deforms us to pull back out of a false sense of independence. It would be as bad not to allow God to show mercy to us because of a false sense of unworthiness. Those who would be helpers of others must accept others' help. This give-and-take keeps us on the path of Christian formation in a partnership of compassion. What we desire is not to re-create others in our image and likeness, but to release the Christ form of their being, to enable them—as they enable us—to follow the directives of the divine formation mystery. It is this mystery that brings us into the trinitarian communion of Father, Son, and Holy Spirit—a communion extended graciously to the entire human family.

Notes

1. See Adrian van Kaam, "Provisional Formational Appraisal" and "The Four Stages of Provisional Formation Appraisal," *Studies in Formative Spirituality* (1980): 468–69.

2. See Adrian van Kaam, G, *Studies* 2 (1981): 117–26, for further development of the incarnational sources of "Formative Memory," "Imagination," and "Anticipation."

3. See Adrian van Kaam, "Evasion of Interformative Responsibility," G, *Studies* 1 (1980): 460; and "The Formation-Polarity Diagram," G, *Studies* 2 (1981): 140.

4. See Adrian van Kaam, *The Dynamics of Spiritual Self-Direction* (Denville, N.J.: Dimension Books, 1976), pp. 384–424.

5. Pope John Paul II, "Rich in Mercy" (*Dives et Misericordia*, November 30, 1980), in *The Pope Speaks* (Huntington, Ind.: Our Sunday Visitor, 1981), vol. 26.

6. See Susan Muto, "The Human Family: Model of Compassion," *Studies in Formative Spirituality* 2 (1981): 383–400.

7. See Adrian van Kaam, "Formative Imagination and Interformation," G, *Studies* 2 (1981): 124.

8. See Adrian van Kaam, G, *Studies* 2 (1981): 316–17, for distinctions between "Foundational Imitation" and "Infant Imitation"; and *On Being Yourself* (Denville, N.J.: Dimension Books, 1972), pp. 173–91.

9. See Aelred Squire, *Summer in the Seed* (New York: Paulist Press, 1980), ch. 8, p. 135; Kenneth Leech, *Soul Friend* (London: Sheldon Press, 1977); and Aelred of Rievaulx, *On Spiritual Friendship*, trans. Mary Eugenia Laker (Washington, D.C.: Consortium Press, Cistercian Publications, 1974).

10. See Adrian van Kaam, *The Transcendent Self* (Denville, N.J.: Dimension Books, 1979).

11. Ibid., ch. 6, pp. 80–91.

12. See Adrian van Kaam, G, *Studies* 2 (1981): 310–11, for an elaboration of the disposition of "compassion" and the concepts of "social compassion" and "mercy."

13. John Donne, *Devotions upon Emergent Occasions* (Ann Arbor: University of Michigan Press. Ann Arbor Paperback, 1959), pp. 108–109.

14. See Adrian van Kaam, "Consonance Aspiration" and "Implication for Social Justice and Mercy," G, *Studies* 2 (1981): 509–510; and "Qualities of the Consonant Life Form," G, *Studies* 1 (1980): 461.

15. See D. T. Suzuki, *Zen Buddhism*, ed. William Barrett (Garden City, N.Y.: Doubleday & Co., 1956), especially ch. 8, "The Role of Nature in Zen Buddhism," pp. 229–58.

16. See Adrian van Kaam, *Spirituality and the Gentle Life* (Denville, N.J.: Dimension Books, 1974), especially pp. 9–76; and "Foundationally Formative Social Presence," G, *Studies* 3 (1982): 133.

7

Blessed Are the Meek, for They Shall Inherit the Earth

Come to me, all you who are weary and find life burdensome, and I will refresh you. Take my yoke upon your shoulders and learn from me, for I am gentle and humble of heart. Your souls will find rest, for my yoke is easy and my burden light.

Mt. 11:28–30

Introduction

What this Beatitude proclaims to be a blessing (to be lowly, gentle, meek) is hardly appreciated today. Worldly fame, wealth, and power are what many seek to attain. The promise of the Beatitude is worthy of consideration, for it says that those who are lowly shall inherit the earth. What might "earth" mean in a spiritual sense? Perhaps it refers to our being of the earth as such, the earth as humus. Or perhaps it means that, in their humility, the lowly inherit the land of knowing who they are in relation to Someone greater than they. Taken in the context of religious history, it could mean that God shall lead the lowly to the Promised Land, the place where he dwells among them. To follow him means to be led from the land of unlikeness to the land of likeness, that is, from sinful separation from God to intimate friendship with him.[1] Because God lives in the hearts of the humble, the earth they inherit shall be his house, a welcome space for those who keep his word and open themselves to the grace of transformation. If such is the promised outcome of meekness, what is its foundational meaning?

Meekness as Gift: The Human Foundation

Contemporary language resists words like *gentleness* and *meekness*. *Confrontation, self-assertion, bold outward comportment*—these phrases push out words that acknowledge human limits. Yet this Beatitude insists on praising all who are lowly. It seems to imply tender acceptance of our unique gifts, another word for "limits." We are not to measure who is more or less important in worldly terms, but to encourage one another to be on the basis of our true worth.

In this light, we could say that meekness is essential for formative interaction—for those exchanges based on respect for uniqueness rather than on envious competition.[2] When we respect our own gifts, we can listen with docility to others who serve as our teachers. Only if we are meek can we notice those who manifest life directives we want to emulate. That means remaining open to formative directives received from parents, teachers, friends, and significant others. Without meekness, we cannot receive directives; without gentleness, we cannot give them. Thus our formation itself depends upon living in this listening stance, which we may associate with lowliness or docility.

Meek persons are also mature enough to let go of egoistic pretenses of power that cloud the truth of our dependent condition.[3] Those who refuse to face the harshness of reality are inclined to base their happiness on schemes of control. It takes humility to see through these illusions and to know that they build false expectations. Pride obscures the transcendent meaning we seek; meekness releases it.

Our mistake is to associate meekness with shy, retiring behavior. Sometimes bold action is necessary, especially when one witnesses to foundational truth in the face of personal and cultural deception. But because one has learned the importance of listening and letting go of pretenses, it is safe to say that docile persons also act with prudence. Their gentleness does not make them pushovers, but it does instill a certain wisdom about when and how to act. For instance, meekness enables one to endure mistreatment without loss of inner dignity.[4] By the same token, it permits justifiable anger to combat injustice. At times it is better to douse the fires, at other times to fan them. Maybe it is wiser to remain a silent witness to truth rather than to become embroiled in end-less defenses.

Meek persons learn to value the art of waiting, of biding one's time until the moment is ripe for action. Always one pays attention to the limits of the situation, never expecting perfection. From the vantage point of lowliness, dominant modes like besting others in arguments or seeking revenge appear increasingly futile. One prefers to lead a quiet, hidden life, accepting the responsibility of witnessing to formative life directives without resorting to violence.[5] Though such a stance may appear foolish by human standards, it seems to be the best way of expressing one's spiritual gifts. Those who are meek trust in a higher meaning profane eyes may label absurd. Perhaps this trait is so highly blessed because it steadily orients one toward the Transcendent.

Meekness as God-Molded: The Religious Articulation

It is clear, then, that meekness does not mean being timid or spineless. It frees us to listen to others and to the reality of our human condition. It attunes us to the demands of each unique person and situation. It enables us, if necessary, to endure persecution without diminishing the light of truth. Most of all, this Illuminative Beatitude calls for a relationship with that which is beyond human understanding. Without meekness, we could not open ourselves to mystery.

Let us look at lowliness in relation to this attraction to trancendence. The capacity to accept our own finitude may make us more aware of manifestations of the Infinite in persons and things. For instance, a newborn child arouses tender feelings in us because it symbolizes our ultimate dependency on others and on the Divine Other.

Then, too, the awareness of time passing makes a deep imprint on human consciousness. What could make me feel more lowly than the knowledge that one day my body will return to the earth? The fact of this passing can compel us to grab on to the day, since there may be no other. Gentleness is an alternative. It enables us to flow with time, not as an enemy, but as a peaceful stream that carries us toward something better to come.[6] With this attitude, we are able to age gracefully.[7] As the years go by, we experience a natural detachment that allows us to attend more carefully to what really matters. This mellowing process quiets excessive stress and undue aggressiveness. We flow with the stream of life that carries us gently to our final home. We abandon ourselves in the midst of passing time to the vast and hidden purposes of the Divine Forming Mystery. Time for the meek person becomes a pathway to transcendence.

Dispositions like gentleness enable us to be formed by the Sacred. Etymologically, the word *meekness* means *God-molded*. Only when docility prevails can we submit ourselves to the divine initiative. This submission is actually a source of strength, for it allows our vital energies and functional ambitions to serve these higher transcendent aspirations.[8] Human dignity is enhanced accordingly, for meekness readies us to receive the imprint of likeness to the Sacred. For instance, in the Hebrew Scriptures, Moses is depicted as a meek man, meaning he could be tamed by God and thus become his messenger. Moses' whole being could radiate the light of his encounter with the Divine (Ex. 34:27–35).

The sense of gift also prevails in God-tamed persons. They realize that they have been given the genetic code that unfolds in their vital dimension.[9] The talents that make it possible for them to pursue functional ambitions are also gifts. Best of all is the gift of likeness to the Divine, the gift that makes us look deep within ourselves, so deep that we find the Other. This sheer givenness takes on an aura of mystery as we see anew how dependent we are on the Divine Giver.

We experience a sense of wonder when we remember that God has formed us in our inmost being from the beginning of time. What a marvel of creation is this mysterious intertwining of soul and spirit, of body, mind, and will, of head and heart:

> *Truly you have formed my inmost being;*
> *you knit me in my mother's womb.*
> *I give you thanks that I am fearfully,*
> *wonderfully made;*
> *Wonderful are your works*
>   *(Ps. 139:13–14)*

Awareness of this rich inheritance calls forth a reverent sense of care for creation. As the Divine cares for us, so we are invited to care for ourselves and others. We are also responsible to take care of this earth, the land of our inheritance. We know we cannot survive as a human community without this solicitous love that emulates the outpouring of Divine Love upon us.

In a functionalistic, dangerously dehumanized world, we respond hungrily to gestures of human warmth and tenderness. In moments when we feel the anxiety of finitude, we long to hear the reassuring whisper of a fellow believer. Because we know how important it is to feel protected, we offer others a strong arm when they need someone to lean upon. In all of these ways we help one another to feel touched by the Transcendent, to see behind all events the careful imprint of his providential concern.

This imprint is seen most clearly in the Christian revelation. God, the Unspeakable, becomes audible in his Incarnate Word. In relation to this forming care, we become like lost lambs needing the personal love of God to support us in our loneliness. For despite our best intentions, we still get lost in the parched land of arrogance, avarice, and anger. We await his Word to guide us once again to the land of likeness.

The Way of Lowliness: The Christian Articulation

For the Christian, Jesus is the model of meekness. He will lead us into the land God promised our fathers at the beginning of this faith journey. As his chosen, in the words of St. Paul, we are to clothe ourselves with the formative dispositions of "heartfelt mercy, with kindness, humility, meekness and patience" (Col. 3:12). By living these "be-attitudes," all counterfeit forms fall away and our true spiritual identity, the Christ form of being, stands revealed. God calls us his children and his heirs as well (Rm. 8: 14–17).

If we are his children, then, like Christ, we must take up the cross of meekness. This means hearing people who cry for help, becoming a healing presence, enduring pain patiently as well as acting decisively. It means acknowledging when we feel weary and not being ashamed of our weakness. Christ will help us to bear the burden. To be like him means, moreover, to bless all creatures, however lowly, as manifestations of the Father's goodness. He reminded us that little children are of the greatest importance in the kingdom of heaven, for they exemplify the simplicity, guilelessness, and trust he expects in his followers (Mt. 18:1–4).

God revered as queen of creation the lowliest of women, Mary. He made her a model of meekness whom each of us is to imitate in our quest for holiness. Because she was lowly and humble, God could do great things through her. Nothing stood between his will and her obedience. Mary humbled herself and, because of this, God highly exalted her. In the Virgin of Nazareth, Omnipotence chose freely to be bound to human flesh. Through Mary, God restored his covenant of love with humanity.

Modeling our lives on Mother and Son, we can grow in the meekness that readies us for a life of union with God. For the Christian, the way of lowliness is but a stage on the way of deification. Gentleness leads us out of the prison of pride to liberation of the children of God. It awakens in us that docile desire to follow his word and his will above all other goods. It is as if the Lord is saying in this Beatitude:

> *Be cheered, my little ones,*
> *Your faith has endeared you to the Father.*
> *So lasting is his love for you*
>   *that he sent me to reaffirm*
> *that the bond of his covenant,*
> *The land promised to you,*
>   *the land of your inheritance,*
>   *is near.*
> *I myself will lead you to it,*
>   *for I am the way.*
> *The earth you shall inherit*
>   *is not bound to this world only.*
> *It is life eternal.*
>
> *Rich or poor, slave or free—*
> *What matters is not your status*
>   *but the fact that the Father*
>   *is calling you home.*
> *How happy you would be if you could*
>   *but still your clamoring*

for worldly goods and listen
to his voice.
Do not harden your hearts.
Calm yourselves
Be gentle towards one another
Be attentive to the good inclinations
I place within you.
See the mundane events of life
as pointers to the transcendent promise
of eternal life in your true homeland.
Listen to me,
Come to me,
For I am meek and humble of heart.
In me you will find rest.
It is my word that will safely transport you
to the land you long to see.
As long as you live in my heart,
you will feel at home,
By happy, my little ones,
because you enjoy a heritage
no one can take from you.

Practical Applications of This Beatitude
in Ongoing Formation

The obstacles to becoming meek or God-formed are rooted in three deformative tendencies. Let us first consider these before suggesting some ways to overcome them with the aid of grace.

Obstacles

The first barrier to meekness arises whenever we claim as our own what is really a gift of God. To live in meekness, we must try to remember that all we are, have, and can do is gift. It is an act of arrogance to place ourselves at the center of being and doing. Only God belongs there.

Arrogance is the opposite of humility. It compels us to treat our limits not as unique openings through which God can reveal his goodness but as diseases to be cured. We find it almost impossible to be self-effacing, as if we must maintain a know-it-all posture that demands a final answer to mystery. Basically, we perceive any sign of tenderness as a threat to our claim to be fully capable of caring for ourselves.

This arrogant aloofness leads to a second obstacle to lowliness, and that is the tendency to dominate others. We feel compelled to be "top dog." It would demean our proud self-image were we to walk hand in hand with others. Instead, we want to force upon them our aims and opinions. If this means becoming loud and demanding, so what? We refuse to compromise our point or to let others have the last word.

This need to be dominant may cover up a deep insecurity. Do we fear manifesting meekness because we cannot face our own vulnerability? Sadly, this stance diminishes our capacity to live in harmony with other people. The more we try to maintain the mask of utter superiority, the lonelier we are. Our life becomes a model of morbid constraint, making it difficult for us to surrender to God.

The third obstacle to living meekly stems from the tendency to see only what is wrong in a situation and never to affirm the good. This trait breeds a joylessness that lacks beatitude. We become literally killjoys, murdering that spirit of lightheartedness that signifies union with God. Without joy, we can never experience carefree playing before the face of the Father. If we do not know how to play, we may be unable to pray. We exude displeasure and are prone to pick fights. Others perceive a hostile streak in us. We are prone to insult people. We lack patience. What flows from our mouths is not blessing but barbs of bitterness. Joyless as we are, we find it nearly impossible to bestow kind words on others. We lack human warmth and seem to be angry at ourselves and the world.

At times, anger is justifiable, as in the incident where Jesus drove the money changers out of the temple. But often we explode with irrational force because someone does one small thing that we do not like. Or we go to the opposite extreme and express our displeasure in glum silence. No one can get through to us, and our anger builds up like a slush fund.[10] If it doesn't erupt like a volcano, it leaks out in inappropriate ways. For instance, a husband keeps a newspaper in front of his face when his wife is speaking.

Some couples hardly have a kind word for each other and operate their household strictly on a dollars-and-cents basis. All gentleness is lacking in their relationship.

Conditions

To foster formation in this Beatitude, we must open our hearts to the gift of God's gentle and gentling love. It helps if we take time to reflect on the many traces of his tenderness in our lives thus far. In these "stepping-aside" moments, we may come to accept humbly who we are and who he wants us to become.[11] Perhaps we have been making an idol out of work, thus neglecting gentle moments of rest, leisure, and contemplation. Have we become more aggressive because we have broken the bond between inspiration and incarnation? Have we diminished the possibility of being God-formed because we are bent on doing? In these meditative interludes, God reminds us that we are not machines but men and women loved by him, doing what we can and leaving the rest to his discretion.

We must cease clenching our fists and open our hands. Hands that are empty wait to be filled. They are ready to receive God's gifts in whatever form he chooses to send them. Such hands touch gently; they do not hurt. Others feel healed by them and more able to trust God. Thus we become good instruments of interformation.

We can only grow in imitation of the Lord's tenderness if we can temper our need for power and become more receptive to others. This receptivity is possible when we let his word become the primary source of formation in our lives. We read what he says in Scripture; we discover what he wants us to be in the writings of the formation tradition. These servant sources of formation, as van Kaam suggests, foster our growth in gentleness and make us more refined channels through which the Lord can release his tender love into the world.[12]

As St. John of the Cross writes in his "Spiritual Canticle":

> *The bride has entered*
> *The sweet garden of her desire,*
> *And she rests in delight*
> *Laying her neck*
> *On the gentle arms of her Beloved.*[13]

When we rest on the Beloved, our worries cease; nothing disturbs our soul. We desire him alone with a gentle stirring of love. Those whom God brings to this depth of contemplative quiet receive his communications in tranquil repose. St. John is describing what mystics call *spiritual espousal*. Vehement longings give way to delight and refreshment of spirit. One enjoys unitive touches of God in the substance of the soul. Paradoxically, in the words of St. John, this "living flame of love" tenderly wounds the soul in its deepest center, but the flame is not oppressive. The wound is delightful, so much so that one desires consummation or the final exquisite joy of spiritual marriage.[14] Such serenity is ineffable. These tastes of eternal life are a foretaste of our final homeland.[15]

These texts, read in gentle appreciation, reveal what a treasure of wisdom we have inherited in the Christian formation tradition. The more we do formative reading, the more we realize that we can only grow beyond the obstacles to meekness by emulating our Divine Master, thus making us worthy to receive our promised inheritance, the land of likeness where we live as radiant participants in the life and love of the Trinity. With St. John of the Cross, we can pray these unforgettable verses:

> *O lamps of fire!*
> *In whose splendors*
> *The deep caverns of feeling,*
> *Once obscure and blind,*
> *Now give forth, so rarely, so*
> *   exquisitely,*
> *Both warmth and light to their*
> *   Beloved.*
>
> *How gently and lovingly*
> *You wake in my heart,*
> *Where in secret You dwell alone*
> *And by Your sweet breathing,*
> *Filled with good and glory*
> *How tenderly You swell my heart*
> *   with love!* [16]

Notes

1. Meditations on the "land of likeness" can be found in Isaac of Stella, *Sermons on the Christian Year,* trans. Hugh McCaffery (Kalamazoo, Mich.: Cistercian Publications, 1979).

2. See Adrian van Kaam, *Living Creatively* (Denville, N.J.: Dimension Books, 1972).

3. See Adrian van Kaam, " 'Letting-go' in Formation," *Studies in Formative Spirituality* 1 (1980): 304.

4. See Walter J. Ciszek, S.J., *He Leadeth Me* (Garden City, N.Y.: Doubleday & Co., Image Books, 1973).

5. For a nonviolent witness to value, see M. K. Gandhi, *The Story of My Experiments with Truth* (Ahmedabad: Navajivan Press, 1956).

6. See Adrian van Kaam, *Spirituality and the Gentle Life* (Denville, N.J.: Dimension Books, 1974), especially ch. 3, pp. 24–30.

7. See the entire issue of *Studies in Formative Spirituality* 1 (1980), for further reading on spirituality and aging.

8. See Adrian van Kaam, *G, Studies* 1 (1980): 147–48, for a presentation of the "vital/functional" dimensions of the life form as servants of the transcendent.

9. See Adrian van Kaam, "Infra-Formation," *G, Studies,* 1 (1980): 137–38.

10. Adrian van Kaam, *Spirituality and the Gentle Life,* pt. 2, "Gentleness and Aggression," pp. 79–137.

11. See Susan Muto, *A Practical Guide to Spiritual Reading* (Denville, N.J.: Dimension Books, 1976), pp. 134–77, for an entire formative reading program on "Stepping Aside and Starting Again."

12. See Adrian van Kaam, "Servant Formation Sources," *G, Studies* 1 (1980): 144.

13. St. John of the Cross, "The Spiritual Canticle," in *The Collected Works of St. John of the Cross,* trans. Kieran Kavanaugh, O.D.C., and Otilio Rodriguez, O.C.D. (Washington, D.C.: Institute of Carmelite Studies, ICS Publications, 1979), stanza 22, p. 496.

14. *Ibid.,* "The Living Flame of Love," stanza 1, p. 578.

15. See Susan Muto, *The Journey Homeward* (Denville, N.J.: Dimension Books, 1977), pp. 199–215.

16. St. John of the Cross, "The Living Flame of Love," stanza 3–4, in *The Collected Works of St. John of the Cross,* p. 579.

8

Blessed Are the Peacemakers, for They Shall Be Called Sons of God

"Peace" is my farewell to you,
my peace is my gift to you.
                              Jn. 14:27

Introduction

This Beatitude blesses those who live in peace with themselves, others, and God. This peace is not something one can muster at will. It seems to be part of the spiritual inheritance promised by the Illuminative Beatitudes. This gift, once given as an inner attitude, has to be shared with others through the goal of peacemaking. In this calming capacity, we recognize a sign of God's own reconciling spirit.

When one lives in peace and develops the art of peacemaking, one lives within the promise foretold here that we shall be called the children of God. This promise is fulfilled in some measure every time we extend the peace in our hearts to those within our interformative situations. It this way we contribute to the ongoing reconciliation of humanity and world with God.

To be a child of God is to hold his peace in our hearts. It is to be as close to God as possible, as if one belongs to the peaceful circle of love that binds the Trinity. Entering into this harmony is a deeply formative experience. Our whole being seems diaphanous with the love and peace of God, thus enabling us to radiate a peaceful presence to others. God may then use us to draw others to himself. Illumined in the core of our being by the light of his peace, we want to share this gift with whomever we meet.

Longing for Peace: The Human Foundation

How often do we profess our desire for peace in the world yet feel discouraged because we cannot keep peace in our hearts and families? We complain of feeling tense. Agitation increases during working hours. Stress builds as plans have to be successfully executed. Patience is depleted by the end of the day. A man takes his troubles out on his wife and children. Arguments begin, tempers flare. Before long, loving couples grow isolated from each other. The coldness between them frightens their children. Soon communication breaks down or ceases altogether. Little wonder, then, that we feel so hopeless about reconciling opposing forces in the world at large when we cannot even reconcile them in ourselves and in our immediate circle of family and friends. We know intuitively that inner peace is a condition for the possibility of outer peacemaking.

What is it in human nature that both disrupts peace and disposes us toward it? There seems to be in our nature a kind of restlessness that is at the same time a longing to rest. This inner dynamism is characteristic of the human being as spirit-in-the-flesh. Our transcendent nature accounts for this continual emerging, striving, aspiring tendency, in short, for our always being in some way restless.[1] By the same token we long for what the poet T. S. Eliot called the "still point of the turning world."[2] Occasionally we desire to center ourselves in this profound peace, not to escape the dynamism of transcendence but to assess its direction. Hence the eternal human questions: Where have I come from? Where am I now? Where am I going?

Peace is this strange blend of rest and restlessness. It is not a static condition but a dynamic quest for harmony between apparently opposite forces, which in reality belong together. Life unfolds within this rhythm of being still and moving on. It is like the ebb and flow of night and day, of sleep and awakening, of inhaling and exhaling, of finding peace and making it. The goal of formation is not to laud one polarity to the detriment of the other, but to live within the creative tension between them.

For example, we receive many directives from the outer world through the sources of interformation. Family, community, culture—all draw us forth in some way. The directives thus received must then be appraised in accordance with our unique capacities to respond to that situation. This appraisal is dialectical in that it respects our present limits while opening us to new appeals. Some conflict between inner peace and outer possibilities is bound to be felt—but this again signifies the dynamic flavor of formation.[3]

The rhythm of rest and restlessness, characteristic of human formation, compels us to look beyond ourselves to this more transcendent perspective. The peace we long for finds its source in this sphere of transcendence. Wise appraisal cannot take place if we cut ourselves off from this perspective and fall into narrow introspection.[4] We try futilely to control reality, rehearsing every stage of encounter, only to lose all spontaneity and grow more anxious by the minute. Peace, again, is not a question of control but of living in creative tension. It cannot be found through encounter techniques, introspective tactics, or pseudo-attempts to gain harmony, as in the drug experience. Chemical dependency gives temporary euphoria but not real peace. What we long for is not quite within our power to attain, and hence we seek some Ultimate Source of peaceful integration.

Seeking Lasting Peace: The Religious Articulation

The restlessness within us prompts our quest for a Source of personal peace beyond ourselves that will strengthen us in our aim to be peacemakers. Turning to human experience, we can locate various moments that spark this quest for the Transcendent in whom rest and restlessness are creatively reconciled.

What comes to mind first of all is the fragile peace of bodily well-being. We say *fragile* because such peace is easily broken, assuring us that we cannot rest there. Though we have enough to eat and drink, though we are sheltered and clothed, it is not enough. The human spirit seeks more than bodily security, though one must not underestimate the importance of filling these needs as a first step. To speak graphically, though our stomachs are full, our spirit is still hungry. We soon learn that we cannot rely on the physical for this kind of fulfillment. Hence, the weakness of this dimension frees us to seek the source of peace elsewhere.

Does it reside in the area of functional satisfaction? For a while it may seem that we have made it when we amass money and material goods, when we achieve our goals. But in the course of life, this dimension breaks down too. Failed projects, economic crises, new discoveries—all make us feel anxious. The peace we had so carefully plotted slips away, and we are left with as much longing as ever. The source of peace must lie elsewhere, if neither vital gratification nor functional satisfaction can give it.

When these fail, we may find our hearts turning toward Another, as anxiety gives way to trust in a Divine Mystery, whose peace checks our useless concerns. In this light, we realize that nothing can satisfy our restless spirit but rest in the mystery. Then we see that neither pleasure-seeking nor profit-making can give us what we need most. These apparent solutions fail to fulfill our need for centering in a source of peace and going out from that center as peacemakers. Only in the framework of this mystery are we able to harmonize the dynamism and diversity of human formation. This mystery allows for the greatest number of differences due to uniqueness, while preserving a spirit of peace due to our common origins in the same Divine Source.

Centering ourselves in this Source is the key to lasting peace. From this depth, we can quietly appraise the directives received from all poles of the formation process and reach decisions that strive to foster peace among all factions. Just as we receive directives in peace, so we return them as peacemakers.

Peacemaking is thus a matter of resting in the Divine Peacemaker and responding to each situation from this center. Only if we see the horizon of divine unity behind each incarnation of diversity can we help to reconcile opposing forces without destroying unique creativity.

In the Hebrew language, this vision was grounded in the standard greeting exchanged among Yahweh's people, the greeting *Shalom*. The peace these people called down upon one another flowed from their living in prayerful presence to their God. Because of the covenant of peace and love he had made with them, they were to cultivate selfless love for one another, making peace by putting their neighbors' interests above their own. They were commanded to worship God alone, to honor parents, not to bear false witness. Whatever bred disobedience to God's law was contrary to the peace he envisioned for his people. On that day ". . . the wolf shall be guest of the lamb, and the leopard shall lie down with the kid; The calf and the young lion shall browse together" (Is. 11:6). When dissent occurred among the people, at least one among them was to act as peacemaker. This person was to be impartial, patient, full of understanding, and pledged to uphold the interests of both parties so that the best solution could be found.

It is interesting to note that the word *Shalom* did not mean cessation of war as such or the absence of trouble. The word connotes wholeness, fullness, health—all that makes for humanity's highest goods. It means being in harmony with oneself, with other people, and the world around us—a harmony only possible because one acknowledges a common Source whose benevolent light shines equally upon all creation. For this reason, we are ordained to respect others and to avoid malicious controversy.

As noble as this formation ideal may be, human nature is such that we fall rapidly from it. God's own people persisted in their disobedience, though through the prophets he continued to promise a reign of peace that would encompass the whole earth. Since we could neither find peace in our hearts nor make peace with others, God would have to intervene in human history. As foretold in Isaiah, the Source of Peace would send his people a Prince of Peace:

> *For a child is born to us, a son is given us;*
> *upon his shoulder dominion rests.*
> *They name him Wonder-Counselor, God-hero,*
> *Father-Forever, Prince of Peace,*
> *His dominion is vast*
> *and forever peaceful.*
> *From David's throne, and over his kingdom,*
> *which he confirms and sustains*
> *By Judgment and justice,*
> *both now and forever.*
> *The zeal of the Lord of hosts will do this.*
> *(Is. 9:6–7)*

Jesus as Source of Peace and Peacemaking:
The Christian Articulation

To find true peace, we must turn personally and communally to the Prince of Peace. Jesus grants the peace of heart we can pass on to others. For most of us, this invitation to be peacemakers does not mean being sent on a world mission but reckoning with whatever causes dissent in our immediate life situation—as in relations between husbands and wives, parents and children, friends and colleagues. We can foster consonance along these lines only if we have first sought peace within ourselves and between ourselves and God. Only then can we reach out to others and the world at large with the ministry of peacemaking assigned to us in this Beatitude.

Some quality radiated from the Lord, some deep inner peace, that made others want to touch him, see him, hear him. All gathered around him—mere curiosity seekers, maybe even informers, but the vast majority were simple peasants, laborers, merchants. Like us, they were upset by the daily cares of sickness, hardship, or the general lot of the poor. One can almost feel the compassion with which Jesus looked upon these lost sheep. He saw not only their tired, sick bodies but their troubled, sinful, struggling spirits as well. He knew what it was like to be one of them, how hard it was to live in peace. Look how often Peter's volatile temper got the best of him! If his friends had such problems, imagine how tortured his enemies must have been.

The Lord accepted such blindness as part of the human condition and took pity on everyone, friends and enemies alike. He made every effort to convince them that God really knew and loved them as they knew and loved their own children. Every effort they made to be good, to make peace, was blessed by him. Because we are his children, God comes to us where we are. Whether sinners or saints, he wants us to be his own in a relationship of affirming love, patient waiting, and peaceful presence.

Despite this invitation to surrender to the Prince of Peace and to let him care for us, we are all like beginning swimmers. We thrust about, we fight the water, we struggle and nearly sink. It is only when we make peace with the water, when we stop fighting it and float, that we can begin to swim. The lesson of the swimmer is a lesson for the peacemaker. Life is comparable to water. The more we resist it, the more we go against its flow, the less likely we are to experience the rest that comes from letting go and allowing the stream of water to carry us. To float in these living waters, to be held by Christ, is to know true peace. Then we can rise up and make peace with others for the sake of the Lord.

The first rule he gives us is: Begin where you are, with those nearest you:

> If you bring your gift to the altar and there you recall that your brother has anything against you, leave your gift at the altar, go first to be reconciled with your brother, and then come and offer your gift. (Mt. 5:23–24)

Interformation fails if we do not settle with our opponents and in our hearts and actions forgive those who offend us. The second counsel he gives us for peacemaking is more subtle. We must not expect to escape conflict, but we are to use it as a stepping-stone to more creative relationships. In a startling pronouncement, Jesus said:

> Do you think I have come to establish peace on the earth? I assure you, the contrary is true: I have come for division. From now on, a household of five will be divided three against two and two against three. . . . (Lk. 12:51–53)

Perhaps what the Lord means to say is that Christians cannot attain peace at any price. There will be times when we have to stand for our beliefs without compromise, even if this means persecution and division. Such conflict is unavoidable if we follow Christian formation ideals. In these situations, conflict becomes creative because it releases our capacity to surrender to the will and providence of God. We know that the peace he has given us as our legacy surpasses understanding. Since the world did not give the gift to us, neither can the world take it away.

The soul illuminated interiorly by the presence of God is truly at peace. This peace makes all the arduous toil of the purgative way seem unimportant. The gift of peace makes the struggle to banish inordinate attachments, distracting thoughts, and ego-centered desires perfectly acceptable. God rewards this effort by touches of his ineffable rest. He knows there will still be many times when we lose our peace and fall back into the old deformative habits of anger, impatience, and useless worry. But we do feel confident that we are walking more steadily with the Lord and that he will continue to grant us the gift of peace if we ask him for it.

This peace signifies the bond between our restless heart and the heart of Christ, in whom we seek our rest. Nothing can break this bond if we do not lose faith. Jesus' love and peace will enlarge our hearts if we remain attuned to the movements of his Spirit, to the aspirations and inspirations that guide our formation journey. Peace is the sign that we are living in his presence—a deep tranquility that remains in the midst of creative tension. We can trust we are walking with Christ and following his direction if there is no animosity in our hearts toward other people. We count on their goodwill and try our best to work with them. If partnerships do fail, we at least try to make peace before parting company. Judgments in such cases are made for practical reasons; they do not touch upon the integrity of the person's guilt or innocence before God.

If we live in the peace of Christ, people may sense his presence and be drawn to him through us. "The peaceful and tranquil soul is like a continual banquet" (Pv. 15:15).[5] One simply enjoys being with such a person. One feels trusted, not threatened; cared for, not cast out; loved, not feared. One bears the mark of intimate friendship with the Lord, the gift of his peace.

St. John of the Cross speaks of his friendship as comparable to the relation between bride and Beloved. The bride-soul enjoys habitual peace and frequent visits from the Beloved.[6] He calms both the sensory and spiritual parts of her soul and puts the evil one, the spirit of distraction and divisiveness, to flight. The soul is thus able to rest in God and attend to his will alone. This activity is wholly spiritual. It is not a matter of doing things for God, such as acts of penance and mortification, but of remaining quiet in God. St. John expresses the excellence of this peaceful illumination in these words:

> Nothing can reach or molest her now that she has withdrawn from all things and entered into her God where she enjoys all peace, tastes all sweetness, and delights in all delight insofar as this earthly state allows.[7]

Other emotions, such as joy, hope, and fear, are subsumed under the canopy of this mysterious peace. The soul enjoys, as it were, a gentle sleep of love, for, as St. John explains, "from perfect love . . . stems perfect peace of soul."[8] God is bestowing upon the soul at such moments the peaceful quiet and sweet idleness of infused contemplation.

This experience of plenitude, which transcends human explanation, is "secret." As St. John says, contemplation is "nothing else than a secret and peaceful and loving inflow of God, which, if not hampered, fires the soul in the spirit of love . . ."[9] Discursive meditation is useless at this point. Such action on the soul's part would lead only to dryness. Now all one can "do" is remain in rest and stillness before the Lord, in quiet and total surrender. He alone can grant the gift of contemplative peace whenever and to whomever he chooses.[10] With this peace comes a sense of inner liberation and an illumined, abiding awareness of being cared for personally by God in adversity as well as in prosperity.[11] Peace means nothing more or less than letting God operate in our hearts without interference.

A spiritual formation based on faith and trust in God is the surest guarantee of peace of soul and freedom of spirit. We then manifest in lived experience the mystery of Christ's peace. We abandon our own will and follow the inner promptings of his Spirit.[12] We act not on our own initiative but in response to whatever requests are made by God in the concrete circumstances of each day. Such obedience is costly to our pride, but without it, no peace of soul is possible nor can we radiate this peace compatibly to others.[13]

Practical Applications of This Beatitude in Ongoing Formation

Clearly, unless we are filled with the peace of God we cannot convey his peace to others nor be called the children of God.

Therefore we must pose again the formative question: What is it that disrupts our heart's peace and how do these obstacles mar our mission of peacemaking?

Obstacles

From the perspective of foundational human formation, lack of peace is felt when we violate the demands of a congenial, compatible, and compassionate formation of self and world. This means in effect that we neglect or ignore the Christian imperative to foster social justice, peace, and mercy. With great detail, Adrian van Kaam has analyzed the question of social responsibility in human and Christian life.[14] Here we are interested mainly in what causes the disruption of peace and peacemaking. He suggests that the key issue resides in our choice of social involvements that are incompatible with our providential unique communal and personal situation. On the contrary, if our choice is compatible with who we are most deeply, and in tune with wisely appraised directives coming from the life situation, then inner and outer peace are a high probability.

The problem emerges when our mode of social presence is dissonant with our foundational life form and incompatible with such givens as family, community, profession, or formation phase. However much we may feel "in" with the current pulsations or pressures of society, we will still experience in the pneumatic dimension a foundational uneasiness, a pervasive disquiet and unhappiness. We may be accomplishing many things. We may be the object of much admiration. But we ourselves will not feel at peace because what we are doing is a betrayal of who we really are. Unless we pay attention to this disquieting lack of consonance, we may fail to radiate peace despite our exalted efforts to do good. Instead of growing in the quiet presence to the Lord that strengthens our social commitment, we become victims of what van Kaam calls social presence erosion and depletion.[15] We can summarize this main obstacle to peace by quoting the following descriptions of van Kaam. The first pertains to social dissonance; the second pertains to social consonance, suggesting as well a main facilitating condition for peace and peacemaking:

A sign of dissonance of our mode of social presence is an implicit continuous experience of a basic disquiet, loneliness and emptiness in the pneumatic dimension of our life formation in spite of possible peace, quiet, exaltation, fearlessness, strength, energy, success and well-being in the other four dimensions, i.e. historical, vital, functional, transcendent of our formation awareness and practice.[16]

A sign of . . . consonance can be found in the steady implicit peace experienced in our pneumatic formation awareness in spite of possible worry, turbulence, suffering, sorrow, desolation, fear, weakness, fatigue, pain, tension, disappointment in the other four dimensions of our formation awareness and practice.[17]

Dissonance in the above sense inevitably leads to deformative offenses against peace.[18] According to van Kaam, it is a serious offense against social compatibility, and hence peace, to coerce, manipulate, or seduce others to betray their providential situation of the moment by involvement in social ideals, however excellent, that are incompatible with their real and relevant situation, position, and duty. If they betray the call of compatibility (and consequently the related calls of congeniality and compassion), they risk losing their peace. They push beyond what van Kaam often refers to as the "pace of grace." To force oneself beyond this pace under the pressure of the exalted pride form or of pulsations of the culture to which one has no affinity is to lose one's peace. Again, careful appraisal of one's congenial, compatible, and compassionate formation, perhaps combined with spiritual direction in private or in common, will help one to follow the inspirations of the Holy Spirit in the here-and-now situation each Christian aims to serve. What, then, is formative social peace and peacemaking?

[It] aims at the elimination of all deformative coercive, manipulative, seductive acts, dispositions, social and political structures in family, community, place of labor, and society that militate directly or indirectly against the fidelity to people's right and duty to foster a current Christian, compatible, reasonably appeasing life formation. Positively, it aims at the development of acts, dispositions, social and political structures that foster and facilitate such freedom of a truly Christian, compatible and reasonably appeasing current life formation.[19]

We can derive from these scientific insights that peace is an eminently pneumatic experience. That is to say, it can be felt in the core of one's being simultaneously with a certain tension or restlessness on the other levels of the life form.

Let us further explore some obstacles to this Spirit-centered peace by looking at the teachings of St. John of the Cross on the problem of disruptive desires. What he means is that we lose pneumatic peace by clinging to little desires or "appetites" that deflect us from seeking our peace in God alone and following his will in our life situation. Only if we renounce these desires and see through their deceptive promises of happiness can we find true and lasting peace.

Wise spiritual master that he is, St. John points out the typical mistake we make of thinking that the problem of lack of peace resides in things—not having enough of them—rather than in ourselves. The other extreme is just as bad, namely, to discover that things do not make us happy and to try willfully to push them away, only to find that we still desire them in our heart. For example, a man thinks that by pushing women away he will stay "pure," only to find that in his secret thoughts he is as lustful as ever. St. John's point is that the problem of desire is not caused by something "out there." It resides within; it is a problem of the mind and will. His teaching echoes the biblical adage that money is not the root of all evil but the *love* of money is.

Turning now to the source of many of these teachings, his book *The Ascent of Mount Carmel,* we see that St. John suggests two reasons why such desires disrupt our inner peace and make it impossible for us to be peacemakers.[20] First of all, he stresses that inordinate attachments always hinder union with God. All forms of frantic clutching preoccupy us to the point where they crowd God out. What St. John is saying in more philosophical terms is that two contraries cannot coexist in one person: I cannot bind myself exclusively to any created person or thing and experience the love proper to God alone. I have to choose which master to serve, for only one can be the primary recipient of my affection.

St. John lists five kinds of harms pertaining to the second reason why inordinate desires disrupt our peace and deprive us of God. He says that our spiritual life suffers in the first place because desires weary and tire us to death. He compares them to restless, discontented children. The more we try to satisfy their cravings, the more demanding they become. "Just as a lover is wearied and depressed when on a longed-for day his opportunity is frustrated, so is a man wearied and tired by all his appetites and their fulfillment, because fulfillment only causes more hunger and emptiness."[21] Such desires make it difficult for us to live in the hope of God alone, for we expect them to satisfy us. We keep looking, as it were, for paradise on earth. Thus we become ready victims of pride and cultural pressures, both of which tempt us to believe that we can find fulfillment in some thing, person, or event outside of God.

The second of St. John's five points is that desires torment us. They gnaw at us mercilessly, and in the process of trying to satisfy them, we lose our inner peace. For instance, possessions clung to desperately soon possess us. We forget that the liberation of the children of God is only ours when we surrender our will to his. The peace he grants is so refreshing in contrast to the affliction we feel when the cord of desires tightens around us.

Third, these self-centered desires blind us. They make it impossible for us to think clearly. For instance, the desire for constant pleasure or sensual stimulation makes reflective living more and more difficult:

> Vapors make the air murky and are a hindrance to the bright sunshine; a cloudy mirror does not clearly reflect a person's countenance; so too muddy water reflects only a hazy image of his features. In just this way a man's intellect, clouded by the appetites, becomes dark and impedes the sun of either natural reason or supernatural wisdom from shining within and completely illumining it.[22]

When reason and reflection are obscured in this way, the will becomes weak, the memory dull and disordered. The will is incapable of embracing the pure love of God, and hence clouds the mind's appraisal powers. Unless these blinding desires are mortified, it is impossible to advance on the way of union. "The appetites are like a cataract on the eye or specks of dust in it; until removed they obstruct vision."[23]

Using even stronger language, St. John assures us that such blind desires stain and defile the soul, bringing it into bondage under the rule of the autarchic pride form and blackening the beauty of the Christ form God intends us to release. We cannot grow in Christ-likeness until these unruly desires are checked by formative detachment.[24] Though the substantial union remains between the soul and God, what is marred by these appetites is the union of likeness.[25] Such inclinations keep us away from the peace God is drawing us toward in the life of union. They deny us our promised place as the children of God, full of his light and eager to share it with the world.

It follows finally that such desires will make us only lukewarm spiritually. They sap the strength we need to persevere in Christian formation. Ours is an on-again, off-again spiritual life, perhaps overly dependent on consolations and only mildly attracted to the steady discipline of discipleship. We really want to go to God through a wide door, not a narrow gate. For this reason, our faith is easily challenged. We may be open targets for exalted schemes that promise salvation. We would like to master God; we do not want him to master us. What matters most is not his will but our own plans and projects. Without purgation and ongoing appraisal of the quality of our spiritual life, self-gratification, not God, becomes our center. This would be hell on earth as far as St. John is concerned. For what difference does it make if we win the whole world and lose our soul?

St. John reminds us that unruly desires can do us no harm spiritually unless we consent to them. Even if we miss the mark once in a while, we can seek God's forgiveness and regain our peace. In time, these desires attain less and less power over us. We become detached from anything that poses as ultimate, realizing that God alone can satisfy the longing of our heart. In addition to reconciliation, what other conditions foster formation in this Beatitude?

Conditions

We can never underestimate the importance of these repentant moments that enable us to see the futility of trying to satisfy our own desires to the exclusion of God's will. Such moments break through turmoil, agitation, and confusion and lead to clarity regarding the truth of our condition. We open our hearts to the grace of God and feel the burden of self-centeredness lifting. We know that with his help, we can find the courage to remain faithful to his presence in the core of our being and to share this peace with others.

It is equally helpful for us to seek solitude so that we can distance ourselves from social demands and listen to God's voice. In solitude, we gain the spiritual refreshment we need to convey his peace to others. Calmly we appraise how we can assume social responsibility as peacemakers without losing equanimity or betraying our commitment as Christians to serve others in justice, peace, and mercy. In solitude, we remain attentive to our own calling, to our foundational formation in the Lord. We know that loss of peace follows quickly upon any willful emulation of his design in another's life. Hence we resist the temptation to outrun the limitations of our providential social call.[26]

In the end, the way of peace is ours when we say: Not my will but yours be done. This prayer brought peace to the Lord in his hour of humiliation. It enabled him to complete his mission of peacemaking, for through the Cross, our reconciliation with the Father was sealed forever. With St. Paul, we pour forth these words of praise:

> Rejoice in the Lord always! I say it again. Rejoice! Everyone should see how unselfish you are. The Lord is near. Dismiss all anxiety from your minds. Present your needs to God in every form of prayer and in petitions full of gratitude. Then God's own peace, which is beyond all understanding, will stand guard over your hearts and minds, in Christ Jesus.
>
> (Ph. 4:4–7)

Notes

1. See Adrian van Kaam, "Foundational Dynamic of Human Formation," *Studies in Formative Spirituality* 1 (1980): 293; and "Foundational Formation: A Socially Conscious Spiritual Formation," *G, Studies* 2 (1981): 315.

2. See T. S. Eliot, "Burnt Norton," in *Four Quartets* (New York: Harcourt, Brace and World, Harvest Book, 1943), p. 15.

3. See Adrian van Kaam, *The Transcendent Self* (Denville, N.J.: Dimension Books, 1979), for an analysis of crisis as formative.

4. See Adrian van Kaam, *In Search of Spiritual Identity* (Denville, N.J.: Dimension Books, 1975), "Introspection and Transcendent Self-Presence," pp. 172–96.

5. I am using an analogous version of this psalm, which is rendered in the Revised Standard Version as: ". . . a cheerful heart has a continual feast."

6. See St. John of the Cross, "The Spiritual Canticle," in *The Collected Works of St. John of the Cross,* trans. Kieran Kavanaugh, O.C.D, and Otilio Rodriguez, O.C.D. (Washington, D.C.: Institute of Carmelite Studies, ICS Publications, 1979), pp. 474–78, stanza 16.

7. Ibid., stanza 20, para. 15, p. 494.

8. Ibid., stanza 24, para. 8, p. 505.

9. Ibid., "The Dark Night," Book I, ch. 10, para. 6, p. 318.

10. Ibid., Book I, ch. 9, para. 9, p. 316.

11. See Susan Muto, *Steps Along the Way* (Denville, N.J.: Dimension Books, 1975).

12. See Jean Pierre de Caussade, *Abandonment to Divine Providence,* trans. John Beevers (Garden City, N.Y.: Doubleday & Co., Image Books, 1975).

13. See Adrian van Kaam, "Radiation of Innermost Peace," G, *Studies* 2 (1981): 304.

14. See Adrian van Kaam, G, *Studies* 2 (1981): 300 ff.

15. See Adrian van Kaam, G, *Studies* 3 (1982): 126–54, for an analysis of "Social Presence Erosion."

16. Adrian van Kaam, "A Sign of Social Dissonance," G, *Studies* 2 (1981): 306.

17. Ibid., p. 305.

18. Adrian van Kaam, "Deformative Offense Against Social Peace," G, *Studies,* 2 (1981): 309.

19. Adrian van Kaam, "Object of Formative Social Mercy," G, *Studies* 2 (1981): 310–11.

20. "The Ascent of Mount Carmel," in *The Collected Works of St. John of the Cross,* Book I, pp. 73–106.

21. Ibid., Book I, ch. 6, para. 6, p. 87.

22. Ibid., Book I, ch. 8, para. 1, p. 89.

23. Ibid., Book I, ch. 8, para. 4, p. 90.

24. Though these terms emerge from the science of foundational formation, I believe they designate a faithful interpretation of St. John's point in "The Ascent of Mount Carmel."

25. Ibid., Book II, ch. 5, pp. 115–18.

26. See Adrian van Kaam, "Temptation Against Providential Social Call Limitation," G, *Studies* 2 (1981): 311.

THE
UNITIVE
BEATITUDES

9

Blessed Are the Poor in Spirit, for Theirs Is the Kingdom of Heaven

Your attitude must be that of Christ
Though he was in the form of God,
   he did not deem equality with God
   something to be grasped at.
Rather, he emptied himself
   and took the form of a slave
   being born in the likeness of men.
                                    Ph. 2:5–7

Introduction

As we move from the Purgative through the Illuminative to the Unitive Beatitudes, we can trace foundational themes pertinent to formation, reformation, and transformation. Suffering can open us to seeing new avenues of integration, which ready us, in turn, for new depths of loving union. These moments proceed over a lifetime and into eternity. Though we can only approximate on earth the fullness that shall then be ours, it is crucial that our attitudes become more Christ-like and therefore more receptive to the grace of transforming union.[1] The two attitudes we shall now consider greatly facilitate this transformation. In poverty of spirit and purity of heart, we are called back to God, who wishes to complete our union with him, if not in this life, then in the life hereafter.[2]

The blessing proclaimed in this first Unitive Beatitude again seems contrary to human expectations. Why bless the poor? Why not heap praise on those who hold power, amass wealth, achieve success? The poor in spirit know they cannot survive without God, whereas the self-sufficient easily forget who their Master really is. Still, from a human perspective, it takes great faith to believe that God's kingdom belongs to the poor in spirit, that is, to those who, empty of themselves, remember him and remain faithful to his covenant of love with them. It is the poor whose spirits are free to behold the presence of God in daily life and to express the joy they feel to others. Thus the Lord blesses those who accept gladly the gift of life with all its ambiguity, who never forget the divine forming and transforming mystery that sustains them moment by moment.

Poverty as Intrinsic to Experience:
The Human Foundation

In a spiritual sense, human beings are inescapably poor. The Beatitude of poverty of spirit thus has a unitive or foundational meaning for humanity. This meaning undergirds the serious problem of material deprivation, and hence it is our main concern in this book.

All of us have felt at times the nothingness of the human condition. Whether we believe in God or not, we can resonate with the Psalmist's observation:

> Lord, what is man, that you notice him;
> the son of man, that you take thought
> of him?
> Man is like a breath;
> his days, like a passing shadow.
> (Ps. 144:3–4)

How true! In common parlance, we say, "Life is here today, and gone tomorrow." It's so fragile. There's nothing to it. Only in the face of this nothingness can we begin to discover the reality of who we are. For in so doing, we let go of the illusions and defenses of our superficial self. We feel empty. We are nowhere.

We own nothing, however vast or minuscule our possessions. This admission of innate poverty hurts our pride, but without it, we cannot become whole.

Paradoxically, the feeling of nothingness introduces us to the fullness of being. If we are no-thing, we must *be* someone. The sheer wonder of being may captivate us anew and incline us to explore these foundational relations to self, others, and world and to all that is beyond us. In his reflections on the mystery of the person, Adrian van Kaam observes that with the emergence of consciousness comes the recognition of how small and insignificant we are in relation to the infinite reaches of the cosmos. These experiences at once strike terror in our hearts and awaken our spiritual powers of transcendence.[3]

Van Kaam suggests that a first awakening experience stirs our consciousness of total dependency on a strange Beyond we cannot fathom. We can resist this awareness by trying, for example, to manage perfectly the small space we occupy or by pretending to be aggressively independent. Neither of these coping mechanisms works. The reality of our dependency remains. To befriend it is to accept our intrinsic poverty. In this acceptance, we can open ourselves trustfully to this vast Beyond and perhaps experience the mystery as basically loving.

A feeling of total aloneness or lostness in the cosmos can awaken a second experience of our poverty. To offset this experience, we may cling to others in an overly needy way, fearful of having to face the pain of loneliness. Rather than running away from ourselves in futile attempts to fuse with others, we have to face the reality of standing alone and feeling lost. It takes courage to cope with solitude, but if we stay there, we may feel suddenly one with all other people in their poverty. All of us are lonely and all of us are drawn into the oneness of unifying love.[4]

Third, to face our nothingness is to face the fact of our total vulnerability. Some people try to escape this pervasive sense of helplessness by bolstering themselves with possessions, but these cannot cure the contingency of our condition. To let go of possessions as ultimate is to grow in the spiritual poverty that enables us to acknowledge our vulnerability and to seek sustenance that lasts long after material and mental goods cease to satisfy us.

From a human viewpoint, poverty of spirit enables us to regain our freedom to be who we really are: dependent, solitary, vulnerable creatures who are blessed in this knowledge and on basis of it pursue transcendent meaning, loving relations, and noble achievements for the common good. Because we possess nothing ultimately, we can and do become poor companions of everyone and everything. Without poverty, we would become predators. With it, we are caretakers.

According to van Kaam, these foundational conditions of dependence, aloneness, and vulnerability are rearticulated in the threefold path of obedience, respectful love, and poverty.[5] Briefly, life becomes a hopeless struggle if we do not listen to our dependency and allow it to become a spiritual opening to surrender. We cannot live as members of the human family unless we foster the kind of self-donating love that sustains us in our lonely condition. Most of all, we must learn to use things wisely as gifts rather than becoming attached to either too many possessions (plenitude) or too few (deprivation). Only when we suspend our narrow views of these paths of formation can fresh, creative possibilities emerge in our living obedient, pure, and poor lives.

It is also true that daily experience as such deepens our awareness of poverty as intrinsic to human experience. Johannes Metz suggests six reminders of poverty emerging from the everydayness of life.[6]

Think for a moment of life as it's usually lived. We go along from day to day unnoticed. For the most part, our lives are devoid of ecstasy. More often than not, we feel overwhelmed by the sheer drudgery of routine existence. Metz calls this the *poverty of the commonplace*. It can become discouraging unless we remember that people outstanding in our minds, like parents and teachers, are not famous in the worldly sense. They never make the headlines; they choose simply to live in the commonplace, trusting in its hidden but real meaning.

Even in affluent societies, there remain pockets of physical poverty where people live below the most basic standards. They have nothing of their own to provide security. Most depend upon charity; some resort to violence. Metz refers to this condition as the *poverty of misery and neediness*. If there is a hopeful sign emerging out of this poverty, it has to do with one's attitude toward possessions. One ought never to depend on them totally. Such poverty purifies our shallow optimism and teaches us to approach things with less greed. Moreover, people who are this poor may in a spiritual sense be more free than their oppressors.

A less noticeable form of poverty that Metz reflects upon is the *poverty of great persons in history*—the poverty of uniqueness and superior capacities for leadership. Those who must stand alone because they have been entrusted with an exceptional mission in history are usually quite vulnerable. Their personal sensitivity and position in society may deprive them of regular companionship. Often they are the brunt of envy, harsh criticism, and misunderstanding. They may even be tempted to forsake their mission by taking the popular position and thus escaping the pain of loneliness. The poverty of transcendent uniqueness resides in the fact that, as van Kaam says, uniqueness as such can be shared but not compared.[7] The unique person must rise above thoughtless mediocrity and the leveling mentality of crowd or collectivity.[8] Persons in history who witness to this poverty remind us also that ultimately we each stand alone.

Metz associates another kind of poverty with the awareness that all is passing. He calls this the *poverty of our provisional nature* as human beings. We know that we cannot rest in the security of the present. Life does not stand still. Our historical here and now always suffers from the poverty of provisionality. The question is: Do we risk living in faith in the face of an unknown future or, overcome by fear, do we cling to security directives in an excessive way?[9] For some, provisionality is almost paralyzing; for others, it opens out into new possibilities.

Related to this poverty is the poverty of always knowing that the end is near—the *poverty of finiteness*. For instance, every decision we make involves a kind of death, for it means giving up other avenues of pursuit. A kind of finality is implicit in every chosen directive. This poverty of finitude signifies at the same time the depth of our transcendental neediness. Metz holds that only because of our unlimited indigence do we reach out to intangible mystery. We realize in a profound way that we are incapable of fulfilling ourselves. This neediness is behind all our longings.

We seem to be on a restless pilgrimage through the universe in search of a final resting place.

Finally, indeed, we must face the *poverty of death*. This last poverty is the lodestone of the various forms already explored. Is death merely an end or is it also a beginning? Metz believes that the awareness of death is a component, however hidden, of every transcendent act. The noblest experiences of human life, like love and trust, unfold against this silent horizon of our impoverished yet transcending spirit. The pathos of poverty is thus the beginning of transcendence. Awareness of our insufficiency need not be disheartening. It is a great relief to know that death is at the same time a reclaiming of life.

By facing the limits of our finite condition, we are able to become more reflective persons, aware of our place in creation yet continually seeking to make our lives meaningful. We need not succumb to blind forces that threaten human freedom or be deceived by the slogans of consumerism. By owning our poverty, we release creative counterforces that encourage us to treat the temporal in such a way that it becomes a symbolic pointer to the Transcendent.[10]

This transcendent perspective helps us to do our job well but not to expect utopian perfection.[11] We see more clearly the relativity of success and failure in light of a divine horizon. This awareness of the More Than is sparked by our poverty, for to be poor in spirit is to long for presence to the Holy. Poverty tells us again and again that nothing created can satisfy us and that we cannot rely for salvation on our own strength only. This recognition prevents us from engaging in quasi-transformation projects that in the end will disappoint us.[12] Our real hope lies in disappearing in the tremendous poverty of spirit that is the pure adoration of God.

Poverty as a Pathway to Transcendence:
The Religious Articulation

The religious person experiences the limits and weakness of the human condition but recognizes simultaneously the goodness and perfection of the Holy who sustains his creation. In light of this Divine Love, terror gives way to trust, misery to mercy, placation of impersonal forces to worship of a personal God. From the dark night of nothingness we are called to advance to the dawn of faith. In faith, knowledge of our lowliness simultaneously conveys the assurance of salvation. Religious experience is replete with these paradoxes: in emptiness, we are made full; in renunciation, we are brought to liberation; in dying and losing ourselves, we live and discover who we truly are. Thus self-knowledge, which is the beginning of the spiritual life, rests upon this experience of poverty.

Religion means relationship with a Divine Other because we feel a lack in ourselves. Were we self-sufficient, we would not seek this Other. It is only because we cannot make it on our own that we must rely on a transcendent reality. If this relationship breeds abject fear, one may rebel against this constricting force or treat the Divine as a malevolent other demanding sacrifices to placate its power. Such was the story of certain tribal religions. The experience of the Holy presented in the Hebrew Scriptures is quite different. Here the Divine reaches out to people in their poverty. Fear of him becomes awe of his special regard for the lowly, whom he himself will deliver (Ps. 41:2–3). In this experience, God is known as a benevolent Other, who has made man in his image and likeness as the highest good of his creation. In worship, we acknowledge that his initiative is absolute, though he can choose the most poor as his agents for the spiritualization of the world.

The people who symbolize God's favor are the *anawim.* Their material needs, which were many, speak to them of their greater need for God, of their total dependence on him. Because they are weak, God can empower them with his own strength. In humble, unobtrusive people, with no power or prestige, there is ample room for God to work. His will would not be crowded out by worldly concerns. They would preoccupy themselves mainly with remembering the covenant and God's love promise that he would send a Messiah. In the *anawim,* we thus witness the transition from poverty as a curse to poverty as a blessing.

To become this kind of instrument demands a full and free submission to God. Abandonment in faith to his directive will is essential if he is to work through us to transform the world. As faith deepens, along with surrender, we know that we matter to

God as much as a child to its parents. We may desert him, but he will never desert us. He is not an indifferent force but a personal parent, who cares about our growth and transformation.

This awareness of God's reaching out to us, of his loving us first, becomes the keystone of the Christian revelation. God himself becomes poor and vulnerable for our sake, redeeming the lost and strengthening the weak. His people, poor in spirit and powerless, are suddenly full of hope. Because they are nothing, God is able to give them everything, starting with his own Son.

The Way of Spiritual Poverty:
The Christian Articulation

The Christian way of poverty begins with renunciation.[13] In the widest sense, we are to renounce whatever separates us from remembrance of God as the Source of life and salvation. Specific objects of renunciation differ, depending on one's situation. For the rich person, it may be necessary to forgo reliance on material possessions; for one who is economically deprived, renunciation may mean giving up resentment of the wealthy. In both cases, excessive attachment to goods or the lack of them clouds one's remembrance of God.[14]

Growth in inner detachment implies not merely giving things up but also giving up the desire for them. We die to the desires and expectations that pervade our consciousness to the exclusion of God. Detachment is not only relegating possessions to their proper place, but involves seeing that in the end we possess nothing at all. Everything is God's gift: ". . . none of you can be my disciple if he does not renounce all his possessions" (Lk. 14:33). This way of dispossession involves more than diminishing our stock of excess worldly goods; it implies also that we detach ourselves from interior clutter. For example, from ego–centered plans that flaunt God's will; from desires that erode our trust in his promise to provide; from images of God that reduce his mystery to concepts we can master. As long as we insist on remaining rich in this way, we cannot truly be his disciples. To gain all, we have to be willing to give up all, including our hunger for power, our need for worldly recognition, and our inclination to be possessive of both material and nonmaterial goods.

As Christians, we are to imitate the poverty of Jesus, in whom three traits stand out: his hiddenness, his powerlessness, and his self-emptying.[15] Prior to his public life, Jesus followed the way of hiddenness, thus symbolizing the intimate relation between the soul and God that human reason cannot penetrate. This way also emphasizes that the poor person never boasts of his good deeds or sanctity but directs all attention to God. "Keep your deeds of mercy secret, and your Father who sees in secret will repay you" (Mt. 6:4).

The Lord followed the way of powerlessness to show us that, through human weakness, the glory of God can reveal itself, for in weakness, as St. Paul says, "power reaches perfection." To the Corinthians, he writes:

> . . . I am content with weakness, with mistreatment, with distress, with persecutions and difficulties for the sake of Christ; for when I am powerless, it is then that I am strong. (2 Cor. 12:9–10)

Jesus' death on the Cross represents the ultimate humbling of power humanly and the ultimate triumph of strength spiritually.

The poorest attitude of Christ, which must become our own, is his self-emptying. Jesus did not cling to anything, not even his equality with God. He chose instead the condition of a servant. Possessive persons, by contrast, are filled with their own importance. They are terrified of giving up control of their lives and trusting God totally. To become poor means to be an imperfect, finite person, choked by many fears, yet willing to take the risk of saying yes to God. *Not my will but yours be done.* These words, the poorest human pride can utter, ready us to enter the kingdom of union with God promised in this Beatitude. We could suggest three signs of this readiness that emerge from living in poverty of spirit: joy, prudence, and productivity.

Joy is a divine gift that signifies our communion with God and our obedience to his will. Joy expands our hearts beyond the dour claims of egoism and inclines us always to share our gifts with others. Inwardly, we live as poor people whose joy resides in the gift of unitive presence to the Lord and communion with all creatures. So profound is this joy that it remains vibrant even in suffering.[16]

God grants his poor the grace of prudence. With the mind uncluttered by possessions, with the will unimpressed by its own importance, one is able to see and follow divine directives in the circumstances of daily life. The poor in spirit see in a pristine way what God is calling them to do. Opposition or misunderstanding is dealt with calmly and in compassion for the pride that blinds the vision of so many. Prudence guides their practical judgments, patience their means of proposing them. Prudence also enables them to live within the limits of their own foundational life form and vocation and not to envy or emulate thoughtlessly others who are called to play different roles in the divine plan of formation.

Poverty of spirit in no way diminishes productivity or what Adrian van Kaam refers to as "form-effectiveness." Because the poor person accepts the limits of his congeniality and compatibility, he enjoys pursuing excellence within these parameters. Limits for poor persons do not imprison talents. They release what is uniquely effective for each member of God's kingdom. Thus the height of spirituality in no way diminishes the exercise of functionality. Without this blending, one risks living in either the extreme of pietism or at the opposite pole of activism. The true greatness of God's poor often does not show up in their lifetime but in the fruits of their accomplishments that live on for ages after them. God, who is mighty, does great things through them. They are but instruments in his hands, ever more refined channels through which his work of transforming the world into the *Domus Dei*, the house of God, can be increasingly accomplished.

Practical Applications of This Beatitude in Ongoing Formation

Obstacles

In light of our considerations thus far, three main obstacles that hinder our formation in poverty of spirit stand out. These are denial of limits, reliance on our own power, and spiritual pride.

Anytime we deny our limits and refuse to acknowledge our dependence on God, we violate inner poverty. In our world, it is considered bad form to show weakness. The opposite mentality prevails in the Scriptures. Jesus castigates those who despise children and the little ones of this world, for they are really the pillars of his kingdom. Denial of limits thus blocks the flow of formation through which the Christ form becomes manifest in our whole being, in our life situation and world.

We also refuse to be poor in spirit when we rely too much on our own power. This reliance shows up in our need to control our lives and to use other people to serve our self-expanding plans and projects, with no consideration for the common good. The same attitude is revealed when we care too much about what we possess or do not possess. We seek power not only through material possessions but through dominating opinions. What matters most to us is being relevant in a worldly sense. Hence we avoid as much as possible the hidden life and seek noticeable proofs of our self-worth, hungry for worldly acclaim and adept at inventing attention-grabbing tricks. Such vanity is a grave obstacle to spiritual formation, making us an easy prey to demonic seduction and miniobsession, topics treated extensively by the science of foundational formation.[17]

If the foundational requirement of Christ-likeness is humility, or spiritual poverty, it then follows that all forms of spiritual pride are contrary to this Beatitude. The eternal temptation we face is that of trying to play God. Just as we want to control ourselves and our situation, so we want to control him. For instance, we want to wipe out any form of pain rather than explore the meaning of suffering. We want to gain as much prestige as possible rather than relinquish honor if it means opening ourselves to God. We know the answers to our prayers even before we utter them and do not feel happy when God's response comes as a surprise. The tentacles of spiritual pride go so deep that most of us will only be free of them in the purifying fires of purgatory.[18] But at least on this earth we can try to find the paths (the Beatitudes) that lead us closer to his kingdom, to the fullness of peace and joy.

Conditions

A necessary condition for formation in this Unitive Beatitude, in addition to acceptance of our limits as unique, promising gifts of God, is to rely wholly upon him in trust and love. We know by now that the blessed life we seek can never be ours if we rely

on the weak foundations of worldly power, pleasure, and possession. Without God, our hearts feel empty no matter how full our
bank accounts may be. Try as we might, we cannot on our own
resolve this primordial hunger of the spirit. It comes only when
we wait upon the Lord and allow him to welcome us into his
kingdom.

To live in poverty of spirit and to be formed over a lifetime in
this Beatitude is facilitated by our longing for simplicity. We want
to let go of the complex illusions of self-sufficiency and live a
more simple life, present to his will in the situation, to his word
in the Scriptures, and to his whispers of unitive love. In our simplicity, we remember at all times that Christ, not self, is our center. Around this center we feel an integration occurring between
our inner and outer lives, between our prayer and participation,
between our solitude and service.

Poverty of spirit is inseparable from humility. A few signs of
growing in this disposition include our capacity to rejoice when
others receive due praise and likewise our willingness to accept
admonition when it is deserved. We realize that in every criticism,
however harsh it may sound to our ears, there resides a grain of
truth that we must take into account if we are to grow more like
Christ. Others are always more astute at spotting our deforma-
tions than we are. Humility may also reveal itself in our growing
love for silence. Too often we feel compelled to brag about our
deeds or to have the last word. Now we are more content to
remain quiet about what we do and to trust that the fruits of our
actions will speak for themselves.

Guided by these thought from Holy Scripture and the writings
and living examples of the masters of the formation tradition, I
would like to share this prayer I wrote pertaining to our longing
for God in poverty of spirit:

> *Lord, teach me the way of detachment*
> *from power, pleasure and possession.*
> *Help me to attach myself more firmly to you,*
> *Holy Source of life eternal.*
> *Transform my vision so I may see*

each finite given as a manifestation
    of your infinte care.
The temporal, like a flight of sparrows,
    is but a passing moment in the eternal
    outpouring of your tender concern.
In my nothingness, let me be present to your
    Allness.
Whenever I grow arrogant,
    remind me of my reliance on you.
Temper my worldly cleverness
    and fault-finding mentality.
Let my rational intelligence
    give way to a sense of wonder—
    for who am I that my God should be
    mindful of me?
Heaven and earth will pass away, O Lord,
    but not your words.
So let me dwell in humble presence
    on this directive:
Blessed are you poor,
    for yours is the kingdom of Heaven.

Notes

1. See Adrian van Kaam, "Transforming Effects of the Formative Presence of Christ in Formation History," *Studies in Formative Spirituality* 2 (1981): 505, 516.

2. See St. Catherine of Genoa, *Purgation and Purgatory: The Classics of Western Spirituality* (New York: Paulist Press, 1979), pp. 71 ff.

3. See Adrian van Kaam, "Christian Formation View of History," G, *Studies* 2 (1981): 512.

4. Susan Muto, *Celebrating the Single Life* (Garden City, N.Y.: Doubleday & Co., 1982).

5. See Adrian van Kaam, *The Vowed Life* (Denville, N.J.: Dimension Books, 1968), pp. 279–304.

6. See Johannes B. Metz, *Poverty of Spirit* (Paramus, N.J.: Paulist Press, 1968).

7. See Adrian van Kaam, "Social Consonance, Uniqueness, Individuality and Individualism," G, *Studies* 2 (1981): 508; and "Necessity of Socially Consonant Individuality," p. 509.

8. See Adrian van Kaam, *Living Creatively* (Denville, N.J.: Dimension Books, 1972).

9. Adrian van Kaam, "Security Directives," G, *Studies* 2 (1981): 534.

10. Adrian van Kaam, "Symbolic Pointers and Utopian Anticipations" and "The Hypothesis of Symbolic Pointers," G, *Studies* 2 (1981): 523–524.

11. Adrian van Kaam, "Perfectionism and the Demonic," G, *Studies* 2 (1981): 523.

12. Adrian van Kaam, "Enslavement to Quasi-Transformation Projects" and "Dying to Human Transformation Projects," G, *Studies* 2 (1981): 538.

13. Susan Muto, *A Practical Guide to Spiritual Reading* (Denville, N.J.: Dimension Books, 1976), especially "Reading the Counsels of St. John," pp. 44 ff.

14. See Adrian van Kaam, "Unbiblical Reduction of the Notion of Poverty," G, *Studies* 2 (1981): 525.

15. See Ladislaus Boros, *Hidden God* (New York: The Seabury Press, 1973).

16. See St. Francis of Assisi, *The Words of St. Francis,* comp. James Meyer, O.F.M (Chicago: Franciscan Herald Press, 1952), especially "Perfect Joy," pp. 12–16.

17. See Adrian van Kaam, "Main Proximate Causes of Formation Ignorance," G, *Studies* 1 (1980): 459; and G, *Studies* 2 (1981): 517–37, for an analysis of the demonic.

18. See St. Catherine of Genoa, *Purgation and Purgatory,* pp. 79–80.

10

Blessed Are the Pure in Heart, for They Shall See God

See what love the Father has bestowed
*   on us*
*   in letting us be called children of God!*
Yet that is what we are.
The reason the world does not recognize us
*   is that it never recognized the Son.*
Dearly beloved,
*   we are God's children now;*
*   what we shall later be has not yet come*
*   to light.*
We know that when it comes to light
*   we shall be like him,*
*   for we shall see him as he is.*
Everyone who has this hope based on him
*   keeps himself pure, as he is pure.*
*   1 Jn. 3:1–3*

Introduction

In this Beatitude, Jesus blesses those whose hearts have been purified through suffering of self-love, so much so that they are able to radiate the love of God to others. Because others see God in them, Jesus promises them that they shall see God.

We could compare this seeing to the unitive vision of contemplation. When our hearts are one with the heart of Christ, our minds are open to the hidden mystery of formation. Our heart, as van Kaam says, is the core form or center of human sensing and responding.[1] All formation movements implicitly or explicitly touch the heart, flowing to it and through it to the current and apparent forms of life.[2] The release of the Christ form in our whole being and world is only possible to the degree that our hearts have been formed and reformed in his likeness and transformed by his grace.[3] The heart is the focus of that intuitive knowing that transcends mere head knowledge. This is the kind of knowing by which one sees God without ever fully understanding him. Only when our hearts are pure, that is, free of pride, can we enjoy the grace of contemplative seeing. When we are preoccupied with ourselves, our vision is too narrow to behold this divine meaning. Thus this Beatitude proclaims that the heart is the locus of transformation. It promises that this heart, purified by his goodness, will glimpse God at least partially here, and in some way will see him fully hereafter.

A Single-hearted Longing to See:
The Human Foundation

Two themes in this Beatitude touch upon foundational longings in the human spirit: one is *singleness* and the other is *seeing*. The first theme addresses our desire to move from fragmentation to integration, the second our desire to let go of illusion and live in reality.

People frequently complain of feeling fragmented inside and scattered in myriad directions outside. More than ever they wonder who they are and where they are going. Is modern life too complex to hope for any harmony? Is dissipation the price we must pay to realize our ambitions? Is there no order or pattern behind these apparently disconnected events? Despite these occasional feelings of being abandoned in a meaningless, spinning universe, most of us still trust that behind this seeming chaos there is a creative order.[4] What attracts us is the principle that behind the many there is One. In other words, we trust that disintegration is somehow for the sake of—or better still, rooted in—a deeper integration.[5]

When life is viewed from this more foundational perspective, when we can celebrate diversity while still positing some primordial unity, we begin to see more clearly who we are and where we are going. We see our bodies not as limited entities to be used or abused at will but as beautiful organisms serving the incarnation of functional ambitions and transcendent aspirations. We live less in the illusion of exalted, autonomous control and more in the awareness of being servants of a meaningful, benevolent formation mystery.[6] This seeing does not provide instant solutions to our problems, but it does help us to appraise each situation with heart and head, trusting in the ultimate meaningfulness of things.

Singleness of heart thus fosters the kind of seeing that enables us to view life and world against the horizon of the transcendent. The pure of heart do not try to short-circuit this process of purgation, illumination, and transformation through drug experiences, flirtation with the occult, or various pseudo-spiritual movements. They know that the answer to their longing to see God does not lie in magical solutions to mystery. What matters is a gentle, momentary beholding of the More Than in the ordinary events of every day. Seeing means celebrating the transcendent in the here and now. It means detecting deeper meanings where others may see only despair. To see is to wait upon reality as it is, not to filter its ambiguity through the narrow screen of our own expectations.

Single-hearted seeing relieves us of the curse of feeling abandoned by the mystery and gives us the courage to abandon ourselves to it. These hints of transcendence redeem otherwise hopeless situations. They give us a new reason for living. When our hearts are singly oriented to these foundational meanings, we become sensitive to deeper thoughts and feelings.[7] We try to respond to each situation in its uniqueness rather than reacting impulsively or closing ourselves off from creative possibilities.

To see in this way, we must be willing to remove whatever sources of formation ignorance block our vision of transcendence.[8] This removal calls for ongoing conversion or reformation of the pride form, a lifelong task that is enormously facilitated by living the Beatitudes. This process of purification is bound to be painful, but the goal of seeing singly and simply the foundations and articulations of the formation mystery in human life and world makes the effort worthwhile. Thus the unity of vision promised in this Beatitude presupposes inner purification and graced illumination—in short, the other Purgative and Illuminative Beatitudes we are trying to live formatively.

Entrance to the Sight of God:
The Religious Articulation

In pondering the religious meaning of this Beatitude, it seems advisable to reflect first on its promise (to see God) and then to return to its condition (purity of heart). In that way, we can understand more fully the connection between the condition and the promise.

The Promise: They Shall See God. What might seeing God mean for humans in general? Surely this promise is not reducible to physical powers of sight. The biblical question remains as true as ever: Who can see God and live? Neither is the promise reducible to grasping God by powers of human reason alone. Spiritual masters insist that God remains an unseen mystery, incomprehensible to finite intellects, yet nonetheless experienced with the eyes of love.[9] No matter how far we advance in the contemplative life, there always remains a radical distance between the Infinite, all-transcending God and the finiteness of the seer. If knowing occurs here, it comes about through unknowing.[10]

Thus the promise that the pure of heart shall see God in no way means that he shall suddenly be transparent to us. A veil of incomprehensibility remains between the soul and God, even in vision.[11] Perhaps what the promise means is that we shall comprehend fully for the first time in ecstatic adoration the utter incomprehensibility of God. The "cloud of unknowing" between the soul and God does not decrease by means of this vision. If anything, the mystery of his being increases, for it is precisely in the vision that God's incomprehensibility becomes the ineffable event that it is. Thus to see God is to see his utter transcendence. It is at this juncture that religious articulation becomes inarticulate. One is to "rest in the awareness of him in his naked existence and to love and praise him for what he is in himself."[12]

The Condition: Purity of Heart. Just as the heart in a sense signifies the whole person, so purity of heart expresses the all-encompassing intention to let God's love suffuse one's entire being and to allow his Holy Will to direct one's entire life. When the heart is pure with this intention, then all realms of one's being (historical, vital, functional, transcendent, pneumatic) are harmonized around this center. One cannot separate the intention of purity from its actualization in purgation. Some chastening must occur before we see God more clearly. For instance, purgation may mean letting go, slowly but surely, of the allure of vital impulses and functional ambitions so that we may attend first of all to the call of transcendent aspirations. Purgation may also mean tempering the need to know God in a logical manner so, empty of "mind," we may really love him. The author of *The Cloud of Unknowing* says thusly:

> Thought cannot comprehend God. And so, I prefer to abandon all I can know, choosing rather to love him whom I cannot know. Though we cannot know him we can love him. By love he may be touched and embraced, never by thought.[13]

It is this inexplicable, increasingly intense love of God that burns away all lesser loves or attachments that may cause our hearts to drift away from him who alone can fulfill us.[14] Anytime we try to bind ourselves in an exclusive way to little gods of our own making, we feel compunction of heart. Compunction detaches us from our narcissistic tendencies and frees us more and more to love God for his own sake, not merely for his many gifts to us. As various spiritual masters phrase it, we become less dependent on the consolations of God and more drawn to the God who consoles.[15] This detachment from anything less than God is complemented by the desire to be more open to his Spirit in all persons, events, and things. Detachment excludes from the center of the soul lesser affections, not by destroying them, but by absorbing them into the love of God.

Thus far we have considered the condition for and the promise of "seeing" God. But what does it mean in our formation to be seen by him? How is our spiritual life affected by the fact that we live within the sight of God?

> *Where can I go from your spirit?*
> *from your presence where can I flee?*

> *If I go up to the heavens, you are there;*
> *if I sink to the nether world, you are present.*
> (*Ps. 139:7–8*)

Nicholas of Cusa, a scholar and spiritual writer of the fourteenth century, meditated at length upon God's seeing of us rather than on methods by which the soul attains to him.[16] For Nicholas, God is Unlimited Sight, the Absolute Glance that falls equally and lovingly on all. God's seeing of us conditions our experience of him. The more he sees us loving him without pride in purity of heart and neighborly charity, the more we see of him, though we never behold him totally. We see as much of him as possible, according to our nature. These different gradations of seeing are characteristic of created being. Everyone who sees is filled to his capacity for seeing, for the Absolute Glance falls on all and draws all to himself.

It is only because God first glances lovingly upon us that we can dare to look longingly on him. Nicholas says, "Thy look is Thy being, I am, because Thou dost look at me, and if Thou didst turn Thy glance from me I should cease to be."[17] He goes on to describe eternal life as a blessed vision wherewith the Infinite God looks into the depths of man's soul, and in so looking, vivifies it by a communication of love. The gaze of God is at once universal and particular; he sees all and each. His glance that makes us be and his mercy that keeps us in being are one and the same. He never leaves us during our lives, though by sin and its deep-rooted illusion of autonomy, we can and do leave him.

Like the author of *The Cloud of Unknowing*, Nicholas teaches us the way of direct and loving ascent to God. By gazing upon him in the purity and simplicity of perfect love, we may reach that "Wall of Paradise" beyond which is the dwelling place of God. Here human reason fails, but faith, building on reason, takes over. Mind flows into heart and we dwell adoringly on God in obscure and loving contemplation. In that wisdom, which is ignorance to the analytical intellect, we *see* what the Father hides from the clever ones of this world and reveals to mere children. We creatures cannot apprehend the "Absolute Form, the Face of faces," save by the grace of God's own self-revelation to us.

His Face, Nicholas says, precedes every face that may be formed. It is the pattern and true type of all faces. All faces are images of his Face. Each face that looks upon his Face beholds its own truest form. Wherever we move our face, God's Face is turned toward us. He sees us and our condition. He gives himself to us that we may know not only who he is but also who we are. The fullness of God's self-giving, his most merciful glance upon us, was cast in the Divine Form of his own Son. It is the Lord who invites us to purity of heart that we may see him and see the Father, the Absolute Beauty, who is the source of all goodness and the object of our longing.

The Heart at One with God:
The Christian Articulation

Purity of heart thus seems to be the basis for our union of likeness with God. Jesus assured us that rituals of purification do not in themselves guarantee this grace. What matters most in our quest for union is that we purify our hearts of any desire to set ourselves above God or unrepentantly to disobey his commands. Purity of heart always involves this humble affirmation of creatureliness and the hope that God will raise his faithful ones to a more intimate relationship.

This relationship is impossible to attain unless, with the help of grace, our hearts break through the bondages of pride and become pliable to the touch of God. The heart of stone will always miss seeing his presence in daily life. Such stubborn persons refuse to offer God the initial surrender that brings new sight. Yet, despite this sinfulness, God wants us to become his friends. He has seen and accepted us from the beginning. Even in our disobedience, God does not stop loving us. So great is his affection that he reaches into human history to heal the rift between himself and us since Adam's sin. To see the Son is not only to see the Father but also to see the bridge to our salvation.[18]

Purity of heart is thus never an accomplishment of our own. It is the work of the Lord in us, the gift of his grace. He can bless those who are pure in heart because they embody all the dispositions that flow from the Beatitudes, manifesting in attitude and action joy, patience, mercy, gentleness, peace, trustworthiness, and self-control (Gal. 5:13–26). No longer yielding to self-indulgence, they put on the Lord Jesus and live Christ-centered lives. Indecency, idolatory, cruelty—such forms of impurity cease to appear in the children of light, since the effects of this light are seen in complete goodness, right living, and truth (Eph. 5:1–14). The love of God enables his friends to give up everything that does not lead to him. His grace has so purified their hearts that they have no other ambition than to do what he asks (Titus 2:11–15).

Many attitudes may prepare us for this transformation, but only the redemptive love of Jesus can release our hearts from temptations to self-indulgence. Thus freed, we can love God with our whole being and others in him. In short, all is of God and for God. One rests in the shadow of his protection and favor. This love is an earthly semblance of that ineffable peace and joy we shall experience in the life to come. In the common life of home or business, in the drabness of passing days, in moments of joy or sorrow, we are to see the Lord as we are seen by him. To be pure of heart is to see his Face where others may see only frustration and despair. Jesus saw the Face of the Father in all of creation. He beheld and called forth the inmost divine form of each disciple. This divinized seeing is the Lord's gift to us. Through it, he embraces the whole world and each unique person, comprehending thoroughly what we need even before we ask. Our entire life is mirrored in his sight. God is one with us and in our hearts we have become one with him.

Practical Applications of This Beatitude
in Ongoing Formation

Self-seeking, rather than God-seeing, is the main obstacle to living this Beatitude, for behind all impurity is the egoism that seeks its own interests first, regardless of God's directives and the good of others. By the same token, purity of heart is the basis of Christian love or charity, that being none other than a right intention proceeding from an undivided heart that seeks the glory of God and the good of one's fellow human beings.

Obstacles

A major obstacle to purity of heart would be any form of what St. John of the Cross calls "spiritual lust." [19] He is concerned not only about obvious sins against purity but also about any feelings or attachments that interfere with our primary commitment to love God with our whole being and others as ourselves. It is best to acknowledge such feelings when they arise; to do what we can to suspend them; to remember that in themselves they are not sinful (for instance, certain temperaments are more susceptible to such emotional distractions than others); and for the rest to trust that God sees our goodwill and will give us the grace we need to love him and others more purely.

A second obstacle to purity of heart has to do with the rationalizing tendency. In *The Book of Privy Counselling,* written by the author of *The Cloud of Unknowing,* we find him telling his directees:

> . . . go beyond your intellect's endless and involved investigations and worship the Lord with your whole being. Offer him your very self in simple wholeness, all that you are and just as you are, without concentrating on any particular aspect of your being. In this way your attention will not be scattered nor your affection entangled, for this would spoil your singleness of heart and consequently your union with God.[20]

Reasoning must be humbled by love if we are to live in the spirit of this Beatitude. We must let go of images or ideas that tend to reduce God to our range of understanding. The vision of God will always be a mystery to man, evoking necessarily a sense of our own unworthiness. Without this sense of God's allness and our nothingness, the pride form takes over and the entire process of ongoing formation is blocked. We begin to overcome this obstacle when we quiet our minds, cease our involved investigations, and worship the Lord.

Such worship is not possible unless we take time to see. Thus a third obstacle to purity of heart concerns our emphasis on being busy to the exclusion of simply being. Do we enjoy the intensity of contemplative moments that then carry over into our practice of the prayer of presence?[21] Or are we so involved with work that we neglect worship? This emphasis on functionalistic involvement may take precedence over our friendship with God. Perhaps that is why spiritual masters insist on the importance of custody of the heart, since grace passes by way of the heart into the whole of our nature.[22] The way of union thus presupposes an unceasing vigilance of the heart and a constant effort on the part of reason and will to direct our attention to God.[23]

Conditions

The conditions that facilitate our living of this Beatitude thus begin with guarding the heart lest we lose ourselves in inordinate attachments that divide us from God. Should we move away from him, we can rely on his mercy, for he reminds us of our true calling by sending the grace of compunction. Repentance marks our return to him and our readiness to affirm his priority in our lives.

Living in purity of heart also implies waiting upon any revelation of God's nearness in the routine activities of the day. Signs of his presence may appear in the most unexpected places. In the midst of a bad mood, combined with much fatigue, we may suddenly feel his nearness in our hearts. He assures us in this graced intimacy that through times of trial and error, resistance and surrender, he has never left us. This assurance of his presence deepens our trust and enables us to respond more readily to his hidden revelations in the midst of everyday life.

To live in purity means taking the risk of abandoning ego control and the false sense of security it beings. We release our grip on life and give ourselves over to the God who surprises. In prayer, we lay our hearts open before the Beloved and experience his immense compassion. Moved by his infinite mercy, we see ourselves in a new light. It is not really necessary to prove ourselves, for he loves us as we are and asks only that we unite our hearts with his will. In the words of Søren Kierkegaard, purity of heart is to will one thing.[24] Kierkegaard compares purity of heart to the sea. The depth of the sea determines its purity, and its purity determines its transparency. Only when it is deep and transparent is the sea pure. Surface water may be cloudy, but in the deep, the water is lucid. No storm may perturb it, whereas the slightest gust of wind raises waves on the surface. In the deep, no swift-moving cloud darkens the sea; it lies calm and clear. So is the person who in his or her heart wills one thing. Such a heart is made pure in its yearning for God alone. As the sea mirrors the elevation of heaven in its lucid depths, so the heart that is calm and transparent with love mirrors the Perfect Vision, the Absolute Glance, of God. The prayer of the Psalmist becomes our own:

> *A clean heart create for me, O God,*
> *and a steadfast spirit renew within me.*
> *Cast me not out from your presence*
> *and your holy spirit take not from me.*
> *Give me back the joy of your salvation,*
> *and a willing spirit sustain in me.*
> (*Ps. 51:12–14*)

Notes

1. Adrian van Kaam, "The Core Form or Heart," *Studies in Formative Spirituality G, Studies* 1 (1980): 144; and "Actual Structure of the Core Form or Human Heart," *G, Studies* 1 (1980): 145.
2. Adrian van Kaam, "Character of the Formative Movements of the Heart," *G, Studies* 1 (1980): 145.
3. Adrian van Kaam, "Transformation of the Heart," *G, Studies* 1 (1980): 144.
4. See Adrian van Kaam, "Relation to Primordial Decision," *G, Studies* 3 (1982): 124. The key question is: Are we abandoned by the Formation Mystery or can we abandon ourselves to its beneficial meaningfulness?
5. See Adrian van Kaam, *Religion and Personality* (Denville, N.J.: Dimension Books, 1980), pp. 3–9.
6. See Adrian van Kaam, "Prehuman Formation History," *G, Studies* 2 (1981): 507.
7. See Susan Muto, *Celebrating the Single Life* (Garden City, N.Y.: Doubleday & Co., 1982).
8. Adrian van Kaam, "Formation Ignorance," *G, Studies* 1 (1980): 458–60.
9. See *The Cloud of Unknowing*, ed. William Johnston (Garden City, N.Y.: Doubleday & Co., Image Books, 1973).
10. See Gregory of Nyssa, *The Life of Moses: The Classics of Western Spirituality* (New York: Paulist Press, 1978), pp. 95–97; and Dionysius the Areopagite, *The Mystical Theology* (London: SPCK, 1940), p. 194.
11. See Karl Rahner, *Foundations of Christian Faith*, trans. William V. Dych, (New York: The Seabury Press, 1978), ch. 4 and 5, pp. 116 ff.
12. *The Cloud of Unknowing*, p. 54.
13. Ibid.
14. See St. Augustine, *The Confessions of St. Augustine*, trans. John K. Ryan (Garden City, N.Y.: Doubleday, & Co., Image Books, 1960).
15. A favorite saying, for example, of St. Francis de Sales.
16. See Nicholas of Cusa, *The Vision of God* (New York: Frederick Ungar Publishing Co., 1960).
17. Ibid., p. 16.

18. St. Catherine of Siena in her writings meditates on Jesus as the bridge between God and creation.

19. See St. John of the Cross, "The Dark Night," in *The Collected Works of St. John of the Cross,* trans. Kieran Kavanaugh, O.C.D, and Otilio Rodriguez, O.C.D (Washington, D.C.: Institute of Carmelite Studies, ICS Publications, 1979), Book I, ch. 4, p. 303.

20. *The Book of Privy Counselling,* ed. William Johnston (Garden City, N.Y.: Doubleday & Co., Image Books, 1973), ch. 3, p. 155.

21. Adrian van Kaam and Susan Muto, *Practicing the Prayer of Presence* (Denville, N.J.: Dimension Books, 1980), especially, Book I, ch. 1, "Our Need for Contemplative Presence," pp. 16–31.

22. See *Intoxicated with God: The Fifty Spiritual Homilies of Macarius,* trans. George A. Maloney, S.J. (Denville, N.J.: Dimension Books, 1978), Homily 15, p. 100.

23. See Theophan the Recluse, "What Is Prayer," and "The Fruits of Prayer," in *The Art of Prayer,* comp. Igumen Chariton of Valamo, trans. E. Kadloubovsky and E. M. Palmer (London: Faber & Faber, 1966), pp. 51–74 and 124–163.

24. See Søren Kierkegaard, *Purity of Heart Is to Will One Thing,* trans. Douglas V. Steere (New York: Harper Torchbook, 1956).

Epilogue
Further Reflections on the
Art of Formative Reading

As our reading of the Beatitudes has revealed, the main aid of formative reading is less an explanation of concepts and more a penetration of the heart. This kind of reading passes through and beyond literal-historical methods to a more personal-reflective approach. This approach is formative in the sense that we allow the texts to serve as directive sources guiding our formation journey. Two elements intersect at this point: first, our desire to grow in spiritual self-knowledge; and second, our intention to let these communications change our lives, if God so wills. These two requirements for formative reading are drawn out further by meditation and personal appropriation.

As formative readers, we try also to enter into the foundational experiences out of which these texts arose. Often this requires more than one reading since certain texts articulate many levels of meaning, as this reflection on the Beatitudes indicates. What may facilitate such an approach is to keep in mind the classical fourfold connection between reading, meditation, prayer, and contemplation. An excellent introduction to this method is provided by a Carthusian abbot, Guigo II, in a twelfth-century text entitled *The Ladder of Monks*.[1]

To show the connection between *lectio, meditatio, oratio,* and *contemplatio,* Guigo begins with a reading of the Beatitude: "Blessed are the pure of heart, for they shall see God." He notes that this "short text of scripture . . . is of great sweetness, like a grape that is put into the mouth filled with many senses to feed the soul."[2] The reader lets this text sink into his or her heart and discovers much good in it.

Reflective reading flows into meditation, which Guigo, staying with the analogy of attaining nourishment for the soul as well as for the body, describes as follows:

> So, wishing to have a fuller understanding of this, the soul begins to bite and chew upon this grape, as though putting it in a wine press, while it stirs up its powers of reasoning to ask what this precious purity may be and how it may be had.[3]

Not detained on the outside by unimportant things, the reader climbs higher and goes to the heart of the matter, examining each point thoroughly. For instance, Guigo distinguishes the pure in body from the pure in heart. He ponders the vision and glory promised those in whom God creates a clean heart. As meaning upon meaning is disclosed, he exclaims:

> Do you see how much juice has come from one little grape, how great a fire has been kindled from a spark, how this small piece of metal, "Blessed are the pure of heart, for they shall see God," has acquired a new dimension by being hammered out on the anvil of meditation.[4]

So deep is the well of meaning that Guigo admits humbly he has drawn up only a few drops. Even so, he feels consumed with longing for the Divine Other toward whom this meditation points. It is not enough to read or think about him; one wants to taste the sweetness one has been seeking so far in *lectio* and *meditatio*.

The initiative to satisfy this longing belongs to God. As Guigo says:

> A man will not experience this sweetness while reading or meditating "unless it happened to be given him from above." The good and the wicked alike can read and meditate. . . .[5]

Because people can perish in their own ideas, Guigo extends the process beyond reading and meditation to prayer. *Oratio* disposes

the human spirit to that Spirit of Wisdom who alone can grant
true wisdom. This wisdom, which Guigo compares to sweet-
tasting knowledge, comes from God, who gives it to whom he
pleases. Because the soul cannot attain this sweetness of knowing
by itself, it turns to God in prayer:

> Lord, you are not seen except by the pure of heart. I seek by
> reading and meditating what is true purity of heart and how it
> may be had, so that with its help I may know you, if only a
> little. Lord, for long have I meditated in my heart, seeking to
> see your face.
>
> When you break for me the bread of sacred scripture, you
> have shown yourself to me in that breaking of bread, and the
> more I see you, the more I long to see you, no more from
> without, in the rind of the letter, but within, in the letter's
> hidden meaning. . . . So give me, Lord, some pledge of what
> I hope to inherit, at least one drop of heavenly rain with which
> to refresh my thirst, for I am on fire with love.[6]

The heart at this point is lifted beyond what feelings can contain
or the mind hold. Until now, the soul has called upon its Spouse.
Now, in the contemplative moment, the Lord himself embraces
the seeker. He does not wait until the longing soul has had all its
say but breaks in upon the middle of the prayer. In Guigo's words:

> [He] runs to meet it in all haste, sprinkled with sweet heavenly
> dew, anointed with the most precious perfumes, and he re-
> stores the weary soul, he slakes its thirst, he feeds its hunger,
> he makes the soul forget all earthly things: by making it die to
> itself he gives it new life in a wonderful way, and by making
> it drunk he brings it back to its true sense.[7]

Guigo captures the contemplative experience in this paradoxical
description of life in death, of vision in blindness. Yet Guigo knows
that everyday language cannot really describe such divine communications. Their delight exceeds what sense and reason can
contain. Hence one can only lapse into silence, discovering in this
exchange beyond words with God hidden and mysterious meanings.

Like other spiritual practices, formative reading is less a question of strict method and more a matter of attitudinal disposition.[8] Turning to the text in the initial act of reading, we pray that the Holy Spirit will open our hearts and enlighten our minds so that we may imbibe the formative meanings in the text and receive the grace necessary to live them out in our unique and communal situations. We abandon the potentially arrogant position of the textual expert and become a disciple who not only reads but also prays with these words. The fruits of this being-with-and-in-the-text flow forth in our actions. As our heart is transformed in this purifying encounter with spiritual literature, so too is our entire life.

Among these lasting fruits of transformation, we may mention the following because they are closely related to the Beatitudes. Increasingly, we experience that deep inner peace the Lord himself promised. We feel quiet within, however calamitous our outer circumstances. This peace goes hand in hand with a joy that defies description. The love knowledge of the heart opens the eye of the mind to the wonder and power of God. One tastes the sweetness of the Lord and sees his glory.

If we are living the Beatitudes, others will sense about us a peace and joy that often helps them more than anything we may say or do concretely. To live these attitudes in today's world will make many demands upon us. Instead of seeking power, we are to hunger for holiness. Instead of living hedonistically, we are to welcome persecution, poverty, and purity. If we are accustomed to being in charge of our lives, it is not going to be easy to give up everything and follow Jesus. Yet only if we let go of ego arrogance and acknowledge our profound nothingness before God, we can appreciate anew these foundational directives for spiritual deepening. When formative reading becomes an avenue of joyful Christian living, it fulfills its purpose as a servant of formation, for not only has it touched our hearts, it has also helped to transform our world.

Notes

1. Guigo II, *The Ladder of Monks*, trans. Edmund Colledge, O.S.A., and James Walsh, S.J. (Garden City, N.Y.: Doubleday & Co., Image Books, 1978).

2. Ibid., p. 83.

3. Ibid.

4. Ibid., p;. 84–85.

5. Ibid., p. 85.

6. Ibid., pp. 86–87.

7. Ibid., p. 87.

8. See the following works on the art and discipline of spiritual reading by Susan Muto: *Approaching the Sacred* (Denville, N.J.: Dimension Books, 1973); *Steps Along the Way* (Denville, N.J.: Dimension Books, 1975); *The Journey Homeward* (Denville, N.J.: Dimension Books, 1977); *A Practical Guide to Spiritual Reading* (Dimension Books, 1976); and *Renewed at Each Awakening* (Denville, N.J.: Dimension Books, 1979).

Bibliography

Aelred of Rievaulx. *On Spiritual Friendship.* Translated by Mary Eugenia Laker. Washington, D.C.: Consortium Press, Cistercian Publications, 1974.

Augustine, St. "The Lord's Sermon on the Mount." Translated by John J. Jepson. *Ancient Christian Writers: The Works of the Fathers in Translation.* Westminster, MD.: The Newman Press, 1948.

Barclay, William. *The Beatitudes and the Lord's Prayer for Everyman.* New York: Harper & Row, 1963.

Becker, Ernest. *The Denial of Death.* New York: The Free Press, 1973.

Beckett, Samuel. *Waiting for Godot.* New York: Grove Press, 1954.

Boros, Ladislaus. *Hidden God.* Translated by Erika Young. New York: The Seabury Press, 1973.

Brokenness: The Stories of Six Women Whose Faith Grew in Crises. Cincinnati: St. Anthony Messenger Press, 1980.

Bryant, Christopher. *The Heart in Pilgrimage: Christian Guidelines for the Human Journey.* New York: The Seabury Press, 1980.

Catherine of Genoa, St. *Purgation and Purgatory: The Classics of Western Spirituality.* Translated by Serge Hughes. New York: Paulist Press, 1979.

Catherine of Siena, St. *The Dialogue: The Classics of Western Spirituality.* Translated by Suzanne Noffke, O.P. New York: Paulist Press, 1980.

Ciszek, Walter J., S.J. *He Leadeth Me.* Garden City, N.Y.: Doubleday & Co., Image Books, 1973.

Crosby, Michael H. *Spirituality of the Beatitudes.* New York: Orbis Books, 1981.

de Caussade, Jean Pierre. *Abandonment to Divine Providence.* Translated by John Beevers. Garden City, N.Y.: Doubleday & Co., Image Books, 1975.

Dillard, Annie. *Pilgrim at Tinker Creek.* New York: Macmillan Co., 1963.

Dionysius the Areopagite. *The Mystical Theology.* Translated by John D. Jones. London: SPCK, 1940.

Donne, John. *Devotions Upon Emergent Occasions.* Ann Arbor: University of Michigan Press, Ann Arbor Paperbacks, 1959.

Eiseley, Loren. *The Unexpected Universe.* London: Penguin Books, 1973.

Eliot, T. S. *Four Quartets.* New York: Harcourt Brace and World, Harvest Books, 1943.

Ellul, Jacques. *Hope in Time of Abandonment.* Translated by C. Edward Hopkin. New York: The Seabury Press, 1977.

Ferguson, John. *The Place of Suffering.* London: James Clarke & Co., 1972.

Francis de Sales, St. *Introduction to the Devout Life.* Translated by John K. Ryan. Garden City, N.Y.: Doubleday & Co., Image Books, 1966.

Francis of Assisi, St. *The Words of St. Francis.* Compiled by James Meyer, O.F.M. Chicago: Franciscan Herald Press, 1952.

Frankl, Viktor E. *Man's Search for Meaning*. New York: Simon & Schuster, Pocket Books, 1963.

Fransen, Peter. *The New Life of Grace*. Translated by Georges Dupont. New York: The Seabury Press, 1969.

Friedman, Meyer, and Ray H. Rosenman. *Type A Behavior and Your Heart*. Greenwich, CT.: Fawcett Crest Books, 1974.

Gandhi, M. K. *The Story of My Experiments with Truth*. Ahmedabad: Navajivan Press, 1956.

Gratton, Carolyn. *Guidelines for Spiritual Direction: Studies in Formative Spirituality*, Volume 3. Denville, N.J.: Dimension Books, 1980.

Gregory of Nyssa, St. *The Life of Moses: The Classics of Western Spirituality*. Translated by Abraham J. Malherbe. New York: Paulist Press, 1978.

Gregory of Nyssa, St. "The Lord's Prayer, The Beatitudes." Translated by Hilda C. Graef. *Ancient Christian Writers: The Works of the Fathers in Translation*. New York: The Newman Press, 1954.

Guest, Judith. *Ordinary People*. New York: Ballantine Books, 1977.

Guigo II. *The Ladder of Monks*. Translated by Edmund Colledge, O.S.A., and James Walsh, S.J. Garden City, N.Y.: Doubleday & Co., Image Books, 1978.

Haughton, Rosemary. *Transformations of Man: A Study of Conversion and Community*. Springfield, IL.: Templegate, 1967.

Herbert, George. *The Poems of George Herbert*. London: Oxford University Press, 1961.

Igumen Chariton of Valamo, comp. *The Art of Prayer: An Orthodox Anthology*. Translated by E. Kadloubovsky and E. M. Palmer. London: Faber & Faber, 1966.

Isaac of Stella. *Sermons on the Christian Year*. Translated by Hugh McCaffery. Kalamazoo, MI.: Cistercian Publications, 1979.

Jacobson, Edmund. *You Must Relax*. New York: McGraw-Hill Book Company, 1962.

John of the Cross, St. *The Collected Works of St. John of the Cross*. Translated by Kieran Kavanaugh, O.C.D., and Otilio Rodriguez, O.C.D. Washington, D.C.: Institute of Carmelite Studies, ICS Publications, 1973.

Johnston, William, ed. *The Cloud of Unknowing*. Garden City, N.Y.: Doubleday & Co., Image Books, 1973.

Kierkegaard, Søren. *Purity of Heart Is to Will One Thing*. Translated by Douglas V. Steere. New York: Harper Torchbooks, 1956.

Kissinger, Warren S. *The Sermon on the Mount: A History of Interpretation and Bibliography*. Metuchen, N.J.: Scarecrow Press, 1975.

Kline, Nathan S. *From Sad to Glad*. New York: Ballantine Books, 1974.

Küng, Hans. *Does God Exist? An Answer for Today*. Translated by Edward Quinn. Garden City, N.Y.: Doubleday & Co., 1980.

Lawlor, George L. *The Beatitudes Are for Today*. Grand Rapids, MI.: Baker Book House, 1974.

Leech, Kenneth. *Soul Friend*. London: Sheldon Press, 1977.

Lewis, C. S. *A Grief Observed*. New York: Bantam Books, 1976.

Maloney, George A., trans. *Intoxicated with God: The Fifty Spiritual Homilies of Macarius*. Denville, N.J.: Dimension Books, 1978.

May, Herbert G., and Bruce M. Metzger, eds. *The Oxford Annotated Bible with the Apocrypha*, Revised Standard Version. New York: Oxford University Press, 1965.

McArthur, Harvey K. *Understanding the Sermon on the Mount.* Westport, CT.: Greenwood Press, 1960.

Metz, Johannes B. *Poverty of Spirit.* Translated by John Drury. New York: Paulist Press, 1968.

Muggeridge, Malcolm. *Something Beautiful for God.* London: Collins, Fontana Books, 1971.

Muto, Susan Annette. *Approaching the Sacred: An Introduction to Spriritual Reading.* Denville, N.J.: Dimension Books, 1975.

————. *Steps Along The Way: The Path of Spiritual Reading.* Denville, N.J.: Dimension Books, 1975.

————. *A Practical Guide to Spiritual Reading.* Denville, N.J.: Dimension Books, 1976.

————. *The Journey Homeward: On the Road of Spiritual Reading.* Denville, N.J.: Dimension Books, 1977.

————. *Renewed at Each Awakening: The Formative Power of Sacred Words.* Denville, N.J.: Dimension Books, 1979.

————. *Celebrating the Single Life: A Spirituality for Single Persons in Today's World.* Garden City, N.Y.: Doubleday & Co., 1982.

The New American Bible. Translated by Members of the Catholic Biblical Association of America. Camden, N.J.: Catholic Publishers, 1971.

Nicholas of Cusa. *The Vision of God.* Translated by Emma Gurney Salter. New York: Frederick Ungar Publishing Co., 1960.

O'Donoghue, Noel Dermott. *Heaven in Ordinarie.* Springfield, IL.: Templegate, 1979.

Pope John Paul II. "Rich in Mercy." *The Pope Speaks,* Volume 26. Huntington, IN.: Our Sunday Visitor, 1981.

Rahner, Karl. *Foundations of Christian Faith.* Translated by William V. Dych. New York: Crossroad Publishing Co., 1982.

Reagan, Charles E. and David Stewart, eds. *The Philosophy of Paul Ricoeur: An Anthology of His Work.* Boston: Beacon Press, 1978.

Ricoeur, Paul. *The Rule of Metaphor: Multidisciplinary Studies of the Creation of Meaning in Language.* Translated by Robert Czerny. Toronto: University of Toronto Press, 1979.

Roh, Father Ray. *Beatitudes: Blueprints for Christian Living.* Pecos, N.M.: Dove Publications, 1978.

Sartre, Jean-Paul. *Being and Nothingness.* Translated by Hazel E. Barnes. New York: Washington Square Press, 1966.

Seyle, Hans. *The Stress of Life.* New York: McGraw-Hill Book Company, 1976.

Squire, Aelred. *Asking the Fathers: The Art of Meditation and Prayer.* New York: Paulist Press, 1973.

————. *Summer in the Seed.* New York: Paulist Press, 1980.

Suzuki, D. T. *Zen Buddhism.* Edited by William Barrett. Garden City, N.Y.: Doubleday & Co., 1956.

ten Boom, Corrie. *The Hiding Place.* London: Hodder & Stoughton, 1971.

Teresa of Avila, St. *The Collected Works of St. Teresa of Avila.* Volumes 1 and 2. Translated by Kieran Kavanaugh, O.C.D. and Otilio Rodriguez, O.C.D. Washington, D.C.: Institute of Carmelite Studies, ICS Publications, 1976–80.

Thoreau, Henry David. *Walden and Civil Disobedience.* Boston: Houghton-Mifflin Co., Riverside Editions, 1957.

Tugwell, Simon. *The Beatitudes: Soundings in Christian Traditions.* Springfield, IL.: Templegate, 1980.

Vanauken, Sheldon. *A Severe Mercy.* Davy's edition. New York: Harper & Row, 1980.

van Kaam, Adrian. *The Vowed Life.* Denville, N.J.: Dimension Books, 1968.

———. *Living Creatively.* Denville, N.J.: Dimension Books, 1972.

———. *On Being Yourself: Reflections on Spirituality and Originality.* Denville, N.J.: Dimension Books, 1972.

———. *Sprituality and the Gentle Life.* Denville, N.J.: Dimension Books, 1974.

———. *In Search of Spiritual Identity.* Denville, N.J.: Dimension Books, 1975.

———. *The Dynamics of Spiritual Self-Direction.* Denville, N.J.: Dimension Books, 1976.

———. *The Transcendent Self: The Formative Spirituality of Middle, Early and Later Years of Life.* Denville, N.J.: Dimension Books, 1979.

———. *Religion and Personality.* Revised edition. Denville, N.J.: Dimension Books, 1980.

———. *Formative Spirituality,* volume 1. New York: Crossroad Publishing Company, 1982.

———. "Provisional Glossary of the Terminology of the Science of Foundational Formative Spirituality," *Studies in Formative Spirituality,* Volumes 1, 2, 3. Pittsburgh, PA.: Institute of Formative Spirituality, Duquesne University, 1980–82.

van Kaam, Adrian and Susan Annette Muto. *Practicing the Prayer of Presence.* Denville, N.J.: Dimension Books, 1980.

von Hildebrand, Dietrich. *Transformation in Christ.* Chicago: Franciscan Herald Press, 1948.

von Hügel, Baron Friedrich. *The Mystical Element of Religion as Studied in Saint Catherine of Genoa and Her Friends,* volume 1. London: James Clarke & Company, 1961.

Weil, Simone. *Waiting for God.* Translated by Emma Craufurd. New York: Harper & Row, Colophon edition, 1973.